A View of Soci Manners in Italy

Volume 2

John Moore

Alpha Editions

This edition published in 2024

ISBN : 9789362921871

Design and Setting By
Alpha Editions
www.alphaedis.com
Email - info@alphaedis.com

Contents

LETTER XLVI.

Rome.

I beg you may not suspect me of affectation, or that I wish to assume the character of a connoisseur, when I tell you, that I have very great pleasure in contemplating the antique statues and busts, of which there are such numbers in this city. It is a natural curiosity, and I have had it all my life in a strong degree, to see celebrated men, those whose talents and great qualities can alone render the present age an interesting object to posterity, and prevent its being lost, like the dark ages which succeeded the destruction of the Roman empire, in the oblivious vortex of time, leaving scarcely a wreck behind. The durable monuments raised to fame by the inspiring genius of *Pitt*, and the invincible spirit of *Frederick*, will command the admiration of future ages, outlive the power of the empires which *they* aggrandized, and forbid the period in which *they* flourished, from ever passing away like the baseless fabric of a vision. The busts and statues of those memorable men will be viewed, by succeeding generations, with the same regard and attention which we now bestow on those of Cicero and Cæsar. We expect to find something peculiarly noble and expressive in features which were animated, and which, we imagine, must have been in some degree modelled, by the sentiments of those to whom they belonged. It is not rank, it is character alone which interests posterity. We know that men may be seated on thrones, who would have been placed more suitably to their talents on the working-table of a taylor; we therefore give little attention to the busts or coins of the vulgar emperors. In the countenance of Claudius, we expect nothing more noble than the phlegmatic tranquillity of an acquiescing cuckold; in Caligula or Nero, the unrelenting frown of a negro-driver, or the insolent air of any unprincipled ruffian in power. Even in the high-praised Augustus we look for nothing essentially great, nothing superior to what we see in those minions of fortune, who are exalted, by a concurrence of incidents, to a situation in life to which their talents would never have raised them, and which their characters never deserved. In the face of Julius we expect to find the traces of deep reflection, magnanimity, and the anxiety natural to the man who had overturned the liberties of his native country, and who must have secretly dreaded the resentment of a spirited people; and in the face of Marcus Brutus we look for independence, conscious integrity, and a mind capable of the highest effort of virtue.

It is natural to regret, that, of the number of antique statues which have come to us tolerably entire, so great a proportion are representations of gods and goddesses. Had they been intended for real persons, we might have had a perfect knowledge of the face and figure of the greatest part of the most

- 1 -

distinguished citizens of ancient Greece and Rome. A man of unrelaxing wisdom would smile with contempt, and ask, if our having perfect representations of all the heroes, poets, and philosophers recorded in history, would make us either wiser or more learned? to which I answer, That there are a great many things, which neither can add to my small stock of learning nor wisdom, and yet give me more pleasure and satisfaction than those which do; and, unfortunately for mankind, the greatest part of them resemble me in this particular.

But though I would with pleasure have given up a great number of the Jupiters and Apollos and Venuses, whose statues we have, in exchange for an equal, or even a smaller, number of mere mortals whom I could name; I by no means consider the statues of those deities as uninteresting. Though they are imaginary beings, yet each of them has a distinct character of his own of classical authority, which has long been impressed on our memories; and we assume the right of deciding on the artist's skill, and applauding or blaming, as he has succeeded or failed in expressing the established character of the god intended. From the ancient artists having exercised their genius in forming the images of an order of beings superior to mankind, another and a greater advantage is supposed to have followed; it prompted the artists to attempt the uniting in one form, the various beauties and excellencies which nature had dispersed in many. This was not so easy a task as may by some be imagined; for that which has a fine effect in one particular face or person, may appear a deformity when combined with a different complexion, different features, or a different shape. It therefore required great judgment and taste to collect those various graces, and combine them with elegance and truth; and repeated efforts of this kind are imagined to have inspired some of the ancient sculptors with sublimer ideas of beauty than nature herself ever exhibited, as appears in some of their works which have reached our own times.

Though the works of no modern artist can stand a comparison with the great master-pieces now alluded to, yet nothing can be more absurd than the idea which some people entertain, that all antique statues are of more excellent workmanship than the modern. We see, every day, numberless specimens of every species of sculpture, from the largest statues and bassos-relievos, to the smallest cameos and intaglios, that are undoubtedly antique, and yet far inferior, not only to the works of the best artists of Leo the Tenth's time, but also to those of many artists now alive in various parts of Europe. The passion for sculpture, which the Romans caught from the Greeks, became almost universal. Statues were not only the chief ornaments of their temples and palaces, but also of the houses of the middle, and even the lowest, order of citizens. They were prompted to adorn them with the figures of a few favourite deities, by religion, as well as vanity: no man, but an atheist or a beggar, could be without them. This being the case, we may easily conceive what graceless divinities many of them must have been; for in this, no doubt, as in every other manufactory, there must occasionally have been bungling workmen employed, even in the most flourishing æra of the arts, and goods finished in a very careless and hurried manner, to answer the constant demand, and suit the dimensions of every purse. We must have a very high idea of the number of statues of one kind or other, which were in old Rome, when we consider, how many are still to be seen; how many have at different periods been carried away, by the curious, to every country in Europe; how many were mutilated and destroyed by the gothic brutality of Barbarians, and the ill-directed zeal of the early Christians, who thought it a duty to exterminate every image, without distinction of age or sex, and without considering whether they were of God or man. This obliged the wretched heathens to hide the statues of their gods and of their ancestors in the bowels of the earth, where unquestionably great numbers of them still remain. Had they not been thus barbarously hewed to pieces, and buried, I had almost said, alive, we might have had several equal to the great master-pieces in the Vatican; for it is natural to imagine, that the rage of the zealots would be chiefly directed against those statues which were in the highest estimation with the heathens; and we must likewise imagine, that these would be the pieces which they, on their part, would endeavour, by every possible means, to preserve from their power, and bury in the earth. Of those which have been dug up, I shall mention only a very few, beginning with the Farnesian Hercules, which has been long admired as an exquisite model of masculine strength; yet, admirable as it is, it does not please all the world. I am told that the women in particular find something unsatisfactory, and even odious, in this figure; which, however majestic, is deficient in the charms most agreeable to them, and which might have been expected in the son of Jupiter and the beauteous Alcmena. A lady whom I accompanied to the Farnese palace, turned away from it in disgust. I could not imagine what had shocked her. She told me, *after recollection,* that she could not bear the stern severity of his countenance, his large brawny limbs, and the club with which he was armed; which gave him more the appearance of one of those giants that, according to the old romances, carried away virgins and shut them up in gloomy castles, than the gallant Hercules, the lover of Omphale. Finally, the lady declared, she was convinced this statue could not be a just representation of Hercules; for it was not in the nature of things, that a man so formed could ever have been a reliever of distressed damsels.

Without such powerful support as that of the fair sex, I should not have exposed myself to the resentment of connoisseurs, by any expression which they might construe an attack upon this favourite statue; but, with their support, I will venture to assert, that the Farnese Hercules is faulty both in his form and attitude: the former is too unwieldy for active exertion, and the latter exhibits vigour *exhausted*. A resting attitude is surely not the most proper in which the all-conquering god of strength could be represented. Rest implies fatigue, and fatigue strength exhausted. A reposing Hercules is almost a contradiction. Invincible activity, and inexhaustible strength, are his characteristics. The ancient artist has erred, not only in giving him an attitude which supposes his strength wants recruiting, but in the nature of the strength itself, the character of which should not be passive, but active.

Near to Hercules, under the arcades of the same Palazzo Farnese, is a most beautiful statue of Flora. The great advantage which ancient artists had in attending the exercises of the gymnasia, has been repeatedly urged as the reason of their superiority over the moderns in sculpture. We are told, that besides the usual exercises of the gymnasia, all those who proposed to contend at the Olympic games, were obliged, by the regulations, to prepare themselves, by exercising publicly for a year at Elis; and the statuaries and painters constantly attended on the Arena, where they had opportunities of beholding the finest shaped, the most graceful, and most vigorous of the Grecian youth employed in those manly sports, in which the power of every muscle was exerted, and all their various actions called forth, and where the human form appeared in an infinite variety of different attitudes. By a constant attendance at such a school, independent of any other circumstance, the artists are supposed to have acquired a more animated, true, and graceful style, than possibly can be caught from viewing the tame, mercenary models, which are exhibited in our academies. On the other hand, I have heard it asserted, that the artist, who formed the Farnesian Flora, could not have improved his work, or derived any of its excellencies, from the circumstances above enumerated; because the figure is in a standing posture, and clothed. In the light, easy flow of the drapery, and in the contour of the body being as distinctly pronounced through it, as if the figure were naked, the chief merit of this statue is thought to consist. But this reasoning does not seem just; for the daily opportunities the ancient artists had of seeing naked figures, in every variety of action and attitude, must have given them advantages over the moderns, in forming even drapery figures. At Sparta, the women, upon particular occasions, danced naked. In their own families; they were seen every day clothed in light draperies; and so secondary was every consideration, even that of decency, to art, that the prettiest virgins of Agrigentum, it is recorded, were called upon by the legislature, without distinction, to shew themselves naked to a painter, to enable him to paint a Venus. Whilst the moderns, therefore, must acknowledge their inferiority to the ancients in the art of sculpture, they may be allowed merit, on account of the cause, to which it seems, in some measure at least, to be owing.

The finest specimens of antique sculpture are to be seen in the Vatican. In these the Greek artists display an unquestionable superiority over the most successful efforts of the moderns. For me to attempt a description of these master-pieces, which have been described a thousand times, and imitated as often, without once having had justice done them, would be equally vain and superfluous. I confine myself to a very few observations. The most insensible of mankind must be struck with horror at sight of the Laocoon. On one of my visits to the Vatican, I was accompanied by two persons, who had never been there before: one of them is accused of being perfectly callous to every thing which does not immediately touch his own person; the other is a worthy, good man: the first, after staring for some time with marks of terror at the groupe, at length recovered himself; exclaiming with a laugh,—"Egad, I was afraid these d——d serpents would have left the fellows they are devouring, and made a snap at me; but I am happy to recollect they are of marble."—"I thank you, Sir, most heartily," said the other, "for putting me in mind of that circumstance; till you mentioned it, I was in agony for those two youths."

Nothing can be conceived more admirably executed than this affecting groupe; in all probability, it never would have entered into my own head that it could have been in any respect improved. But when I first had the happiness of becoming acquainted with Mr. Lock, a period of my life which I shall always recollect with peculiar pleasure, I remember my conversing with him upon this subject; and that Gentleman, after mentioning the execution of this piece, in the highest terms of praise, observed that, had the figure of Laocoon been *alone*, it would have been perfect. As a man suffering the most excruciating bodily pain with becoming fortitude, it admits of no improvement; his proportions, his form, his action, his expression, are exquisite. But when his sons appear, he is no longer an insulated, suffering individual, who, when he has met pain and death with dignity, has done all that could be expected from man; he commences *father*, and a much wider field is opened to the artist. We expect the deepest pathos in the exhibition of the sublimest character that art can offer to the contemplation of the human mind: A father forgetting pain, and instant death, to save his children. This Sublime and Pathetic the artist either did not see, or despaired of attaining. Laocoon's sufferings are merely corporal; he is deaf to the cries of his agonizing children, who are calling on him for assistance. But had he been throwing a look of anguish upon his sons, had he seemed to have forgotten his own sufferings in theirs, he would have commanded the sympathy of the spectator in a much higher degree. On the whole, Mr. Lock was of opinion, that the execution of this groupe is perfect, but that the conception is not equal to the execution. I shall leave it to others to decide whether Mr. Lock, in these observations, spoke like a man of taste: I am sure he spoke like a father. I have sensibility to feel the beauty and justness of the remark, though I had not the ingenuity to make it.

It is disputed whether this groupe was formed from Virgil's description of the death of Laocoon and his sons, or the description made from the groupe; it is evident, from their minute resemblance, that one or other must have been the case. The Poet mentions a circumstance, which could not be represented by the sculptor; he says that, although every other person around sought safety by flight, the father was attacked by the serpents, while he was advancing to the assistance of his sons—

—auxilio subeuntem ac tela ferentem.

This deficiency in the sculptor's art would have been finely supplied by the improvement which Mr. Lock proposed.

Reflecting on the dreadful condition of three persons entangled in the horrid twinings of serpents, and after contemplating the varied anguish so strongly expressed in their countenances, it is a relief to turn the eye to the heavenly figure of the Apollo. To form an adequate idea of the beauty of this statue, it is absolutely necessary to see it. With all the advantages of colour and life, the human form never appeared so beautiful; and we never can sufficiently admire the artist, who has endowed marble with a finer expression of grace, dignity, and understanding, than ever were seen in living features. In the forming of this inimitable figure, the artist seems to have wrought after an ideal form of beauty, superior to any in nature, and which existed only in his own imagination.

The admired statue of Antinous is in the same Court. Nothing can be more light, elegant, and easy; the proportions are exact, and the execution perfect. It is an exquisite representation of the most beautiful youth that ever lived.

The statue of Apollo represents something superior, and the emotions it excites are all of the sublime cast.

LETTER XLVII.

The present Pope, who has assumed the name of Pius the Sixth, is a tall, well-made man, about sixty years of age, but retaining in his look all the freshness of a much earlier period of life. He lays a greater stress on the ceremonious part of religion than his predecessor Ganganelli, in whose reign a great relaxation of church-discipline is thought to have taken place. The late Pope was a man of moderation, good sense, and simplicity of manners; and could not go through all the ostentatious parade which his station required, without reluctance, and marks of disgust. He knew that the opinions of mankind had undergone a very great change since those ceremonies were established; and that some of the most respectable of the spectators considered as perfectly frivolous many things which formerly had been held as sacred. A man of good sense may seem to lay the greatest weight on ceremonies which he himself considers as ridiculous, provided he thinks the people, in whose sight he goes through them, are impressed with a conviction of their importance; but if he knows that some of the beholders are entirely of a different way of thinking, he will be strongly tempted to evince, by some means or other, that he despises the fooleries he performs, as much as any of them. This, in all probability, was the case with Ganganelli; who, besides, was an enemy to fraud and hypocrisy of every kind. But, however remiss he may have been with regard to the etiquette of his spiritual functions, every body acknowledges his diligence and activity in promoting the temporal good of his subjects. He did all in his power to revive trade, and to encourage manufactures and industry of every kind. He built no churches, but he repaired the roads all over the ecclesiastical state; he restrained the malevolence of bigots, removed absurd prejudices, and promoted sentiments of charity and good-will to mankind in general, without excepting even heretics. His enemies, the Jesuits, with an intention to make him odious in the eyes of his own subjects, gave him the name of the Protestant Pope. If they supposed that this calumny would be credited, on account of the conduct above mentioned, they at once paid the highest compliment to the Pope and the Protestant religion. The careless manner in which Ganganelli performed certain functions, and the general tenour of his life and sentiments, were lamented by politicians, as well as by bigots. However frivolous the former might think many ceremonies in themselves, they still considered them as of political importance, in such a government as that of Rome; and the Conclave held on the death of the late Pope, are thought to have been in some degree influenced by such considerations in chusing his successor. The present Pope, before he was raised to that dignity, was considered as a firm believer in all the tenets of the Roman Church, and a strict and scrupulous observer of all its injunctions and ceremonials. As his pretensions, in point of family, fortune, and connexions, were smaller than those of most of his brother cardinals, it is the more probable that he owed his elevation to this part of his character, which rendered him a proper person to check the progress of abuses that had been entirely neglected by the late Pope; under whose administration free-thinking was said to have been countenanced, Protestantism in general regarded with diminished abhorrence, and the Calvinists in particular treated with a degree of indulgence, to which their inveterate enmity to the church of Rome gave them no title. Several instances of this are enumerated, and one in particular, which, I dare say, you will think a stronger proof of the late Pope's good sense and good humour, than of that negligence to which his enemies imputed it.

A Scotch presbyterian having heated his brain, by reading the Book of Martyrs, the cruelties of the Spanish Inquisition, and the Histories of all the persecutions that ever were raised by the Roman Catholics against the Protestants, was seized with a dread, that the same horrors were just about to be renewed. This terrible idea disturbed his imagination day and night; he thought of nothing but racks and scaffolds; and, on one occasion, he dreamt that there was a continued train of bonfires, with a tar-barrel and a Protestant in each, all the way from Smithfield to St. Andrews.

He communicated the anxiety and distress of his mind to a worthy sensible clergyman who lived in the neighbourhood. This gentleman took great pains to quiet his fears, proving to him, by strong and obvious arguments, that there was little or no danger of such an event as he dreaded. These reasonings had a powerful effect while they were delivering, but the impression did not last, and was always effaced by a few pages of the Book of Martyrs. As soon as the clergyman remarked this, he advised the relations to remove that, and every book which treated of persecution or martyrdom, entirely out of the poor man's reach. This was done accordingly, and books of a less gloomy complexion were substituted in their place; but as all of them formed a strong contrast with the colour of his mind, he could not bear their perusal, but betook himself to the study of the Bible, which was the only book of his ancient library which had been left; and so strong a hold had his former studies taken of his imagination, that he could relish no part of the Bible, except the Revelation of St. John, a great part of which, he thought, referred to the whore of Babylon, or in other words, the Pope of Rome. This part of the scripture he perused continually with unabating ardor and delight. His friend the clergyman, having observed this, took occasion to say, that every part of the Holy Bible was, without doubt, most sublime, and wonderfully instructive; yet he was surprised to see that he limited his studies entirely to the last book, and neglected all the rest. To which the other replied, That *he* who was a divine, and a man of learning, might, with propriety, read all the sacred volume from beginning to end; but, for his own part, he thought proper to confine himself to what he could understand; and *therefore*, though he had a due respect for all the scripture, he acknowledged he gave a preference to the Revelation of St. John. This answer entirely satisfied the clergyman; he did not think it expedient to question him any farther; he took his leave, after having requested the people of the family with whom this person lived, to have a watchful eye on their relation. In the mean time, this poor man's terrors, with regard to the revival of popery and persecution, daily augmented; and nature, in all probability, would have sunk under the weight of such accumulated anxiety, had not a thought occurred which relieved his mind in an instant, by suggesting an infallible method of preventing all the evils which his imagination had been brooding over for so long a time. The happy idea which afforded him so much comfort, was no other, than that he should immediately go to Rome, and convert the Pope from the Roman Catholic to the Presbyterian religion. The moment he hit on this fortunate expedient, he felt at once the strongest impulse to undertake the task, and the fullest conviction that his undertaking would be crowned with success; it is no wonder, therefore, that his countenance threw off its former gloom, and that all his features brightened with the heart-felt thrillings of happiness and self-applause. While his relations congratulated each other on this agreeable change, the exulting visionary, without communicating his design to any mortal, set out for London, took his passage to Leghorn, and, in a short time after, arrived in perfect health of body, and in exalted spirits, at Rome.

He directly applied to an ecclesiastic of his own country, of whose obliging temper he had previously heard, and whom he considered as a proper person to procure him an interview necessary for the accomplishment of his project. He informed that gentleman, that he earnestly wished to have a conference with the Pope, on a business of infinite importance, and which admitted of no delay. It was not difficult to perceive the state of this poor man's mind; the good-natured ecclesiastic endeavoured to sooth and amuse him, putting off the conference till a distant day; in hopes that means might be fallen on, during the interval, to prevail on him to return to his own country. A few days after this, however, he happened to go to St. Peter's church, at the very time when his Holiness was performing some religious ceremony. At this sight our impatient missionary felt all his passions inflamed with irresistible ardour; he could no longer wait for the expected conference, but bursting out with zealous indignation, he exclaimed, "O thou beast of nature, with seven heads and ten horns! thou mother of harlots, arrayed in purple and scarlet, and decked with gold and precious stones and pearls! throw away the golden cup of abominations, and the filthiness of thy fornication!"

You may easily imagine the astonishment and hubbub that such an apostrophe, from such a person, in such a place, would occasion; he was immediately carried to prison by the Swiss halberdiers.

When it was known that he was a British subject, some who understood English were ordered to attend his examination. The first question asked of him was, "What had brought him to Rome?" He answered, "To anoint the eyes of the scarlet whore with eye-salve, that she might see her wickedness." They asked, "Who he meant by the scarlet whore?" He answered, "Who else could he mean, but her who sitteth upon seven mountains, who hath seduced the kings of the earth to commit fornication, and who hath gotten drunk with the blood of the saints, and the blood of the martyrs?" Many other questions were asked, and such provoking answers returned, that some suspected the man affected madness, that he might give vent to his rancour and petulance with impunity; and they were for condemning him to the gallies, that he might be taught more sense, and better manners. But when they communicated their sentiments to Clement the Fourteenth, he said, with great good humour, "That he never had heard of any body whose understanding, or politeness, had been much improved at that school; that although the poor man's first address had been a little rough and abrupt, yet he could not help considering himself as obliged to him for his good intentions, and for his undertaking such a long journey with a view to do good." He afterwards gave orders to treat the man with gentleness while he remained in confinement, and to put him on board the first ship bound from Civita Vecchia to England, defraying the expence of his passage. However humane and reasonable this conduct may be thought by many, there were people who condemned it as an injudicious piece of lenity, which might have a tendency to sink the dignity of the sacred office, and expose it to future insults. If such behaviour as this did not pass without blame, it may be easily supposed, that few of the late Pope's actions escaped uncensured; and many who loved the easy amiable dispositions of the man, were of opinion, that the spirit of the times required a different character on the Papal throne. This idea prevailed among the Cardinals at the late election, and the Conclave is supposed to have fixed on Cardinal Braschi to be Pope, from the same motive that the Roman senate sometimes chose a Dictator to restore and enforce the ancient discipline.

LETTER XLVIII.

Rome.

Pius the Sixth performs all the religious functions of his office in the most solemn manner; not only on public and extraordinary occasions, but also in the most common acts of devotion. I happened lately to be at St. Peter's church, when there was scarcely any other body there; while I lounged from chapel to chapel, looking at the sculpture and paintings, the Pope entered with a very few attendants; when he came to the statue of St. Peter, he was not satisfied with bowing, which is the usual mark of respect shewn to that image; or with kneeling, which is performed by more zealous persons; or with kissing the foot, which I formerly imagined concluded the climax of devotion; he bowed, he knelt, he kissed the foot, and then he rubbed his brow and his whole head with every mark of humility, fervour, and adoration, upon the sacred stump.—It is no more, one half of the foot having been long since worn away by the lips of the pious; and if the example of his Holiness is universally imitated, nothing but a miracle can prevent the leg, thigh, and other parts from meeting with the same fate. This uncommon appearance of zeal in the Pope, is not imputed to hypocrisy or to policy, but is supposed to proceed entirely from a conviction of the efficacy of those holy frictions; an opinion which has given people a much higher idea of the strength of his faith, than of his understanding. This being jubilee year, he may possibly think a greater appearance of devotion necessary now, than at any other time. The first jubilee was instituted by Boniface the Eighth, in the year 1300. Many ceremonies and institutions of the Roman Catholic church are founded on those of the old Heathens. This is evidently an imitation of the Roman secular games, which were exhibited every hundredth year in honour of the gods[1]; they lasted three days and three nights; they were attended with great pomp, and drew vast numbers of people to Rome, from all parts of Italy, and the most distant provinces. Boniface, recollecting this, determined to institute something analogous, which would immortalize his own name, and promote the interest of the Roman Catholic religion in general, and that of the city of Rome in particular. He embraced the favourable opportunity which the beginning of a century presented; he invented a few extraordinary ceremonies, and declared the year 1300 the first jubilee year, during which he assured mankind, that heaven would be in a particular manner propitious, in granting indulgences, and remission of sins, to all who should come to Rome, and attend the functions there to be performed, at this fortunate period, which was not to occur again for a hundred years. This drew a great concourse of wealthy sinners to Rome; and the extraordinary circulation of money it occasioned, was strongly felt all over the Pope's dominions. Clement the Sixth, regretting that these advantages should occur so seldom, abridged the period, and declared there would be a jubilee every fifty years; the second was accordingly celebrated in the year 1350. Sixtus the Fifth, imagining that the interval was still too long, once more retrenched the half; and ever since there has been a jubilee every twenty-fifth year[2]. It is not likely that any future Pope will think of shortening this period; if any alteration were again to take place, it most probably would be, to restore the ancient period of fifty or a hundred years; for, instead of the wealthy pilgrims who flocked to Rome from every quarter of Christendom, ninety-nine in a hundred of those who come now, are supported by alms during their journey, or are barely able to defray their own expences by the strictest œconomy; and his Holiness is supposed at present to derive no other advantage from the uncommon fatigue he is obliged to go through on the jubilee year, except the satisfaction he feels, in reflecting on the benefit his labours confer on the souls of the beggars, and other travellers, who resort from all corners of Italy to Rome, on this blessed occasion. The States which border on the Pope's dominions, suffer many temporal inconveniencies from the zeal of the peasants and manufacturers, the greater part of whom still make a point of visiting St. Peter's on the jubilee year; the loss sustained by the countries which such emigrants abandon, is not balanced by any advantage transferred to that to which they resort; the good arising on the whole, being entirely of a spiritual nature. By far the greater number of pilgrims come from the kingdom of Naples, whose inhabitants are said to be of a very devout and very amorous disposition. The first prompts them to go to Rome in search of that absolution which the second renders necessary; and on the year of jubilee, when indulgences are to be had at an easier rate than at any other time, those who can afford it generally carry away such a stock, as not only is sufficient to clear old scores, but will also serve as an indemnifying fund for future transgressions.

There is one door into the church of St. Peter's, which is called the Holy Door. This is always walled up, except on this distinguished year; and even then no person is permitted to enter by it, but in the humblest posture. The pilgrims, and many others, prefer crawling into the church upon their knees, by this door; to walking in, the usual way, by any other. I was present at the shutting up of this Holy Door. The Pope being seated on a raised seat, or kind of throne, surrounded by Cardinals and other ecclesiastics, an anthem was sung, accompanied by all sorts of musical instruments. During the performance, his Holiness descended from the throne, with a golden trowel in his hand, placed the first brick, and applied some mortar; he then returned to his seat, and the door was instantly built up by more expert, though less hallowed, workmen; and will remain as it is now, till the beginning of the nineteenth century, when it will be again opened, by the Pope then in being, with the same solemnity that it has been now shut. Though his Holiness places but a single brick, yet it is very remarkable that this never fails to communicate its influence, in such a rapid and powerful manner, that, within about an hour, or at most an hour and a half, all the other bricks, which form the wall of the Holy Door, acquire an equal degree of sanctity with that placed by the Pope's own hands. The common people and pilgrims are well acquainted with this wonderful effect. At the beginning of this Jubilee-year, when the late wall was thrown down, men, women, and children scrambled and fought for the fragments of the bricks and mortar, with the same eagerness which less enlightened mobs display, on days of public rejoicing, when handfuls of money are thrown among them. I have been often assured that those pieces of brick, besides their sanctity, have also the virtue of curing many of the most obstinate diseases: and, if newspapers were permitted at Rome, there is not the least reason to doubt, that those cures would be attested publicly by the patients, in a manner as satisfactory and convincing as are the cures performed daily by the pills, powders, drops, and balsams advertised in the London newspapers. After the shutting of the Holy Door, mass was celebrated at midnight; and the ceremony was attended by vast multitudes of people. For my own part, I suspended my curiosity till next day, which was Christmas-day, when I returned again to St. Peter's church, and saw the Pope perform mass on that solemn occasion. His Holiness went through all the evolutions of the ceremony with an address and flexibility of body, which are rarely to be found in those who wear the tiara; who are, generally speaking, men bowing under the load of years and infirmities. His present Holiness has hitherto suffered from neither. His features are regular, and he has a fine countenance; his person is straight, and his movements graceful. His leg and foot are remarkably well made, and always ornamented with silk stockings, and red slippers, of the most delicate construction. Notwithstanding that the papal uniforms are by no means calculated to set off the person to the greatest advantage, yet the peculiar neatness with which they are put on, and the nice adjustment of their most minute parts, sufficiently prove that his present Holiness is not insensible of the charms of his person, or unsolicitous about his external ornaments. Though verging towards the winter of life, his cheeks still glow with autumnal roses, which, at a little distance, appear as blooming as those of the spring. If he himself were less clear-sighted than he seems to be, to the beauties of his face and person, he could not also be deaf to the voices of the women, who break out into exclamations, in praise of both, as often as he appears in public. On a public occasion, lately, as he was carried through a particular street, a young woman at a window exclaimed, "Quanto e bello! O quanto e bello!" and was immediately answered by a zealous old lady at the window opposite, who, folding her hands in each other, and raising her eyes to heaven, cried out, with a mixture of love for his person, and veneration for his sacred office,

"Tanto e bello, quanto e santo!" When we know that such a quantity of incense is daily burnt under his sacred nostrils, we ought not to be astonished, though we should find his brain, on some occasions, a little intoxicated.

Vanity is a very comfortable failing; and has such an universal power over mankind, that not only the gay blossoms of youth, but even the shrivelled bosom of age, and the contracted heart of bigotry, open, expand, and display strong marks of sensibility under its influence.

After mass, the Pope gave the benediction to the people assembled in the Grand Court, before the church of St. Peter's. It was a remarkably fine day; an immense multitude filled that spacious and magnificent area; the horse and foot guards were drawn up in their most showy uniform. The Pope, seated in an open, portable chair, in all the splendour which his wardrobe could give, with the tiara on his head, was carried out of a large window, which opens on a balcony in the front of St. Peter's. The silk hangings and gold trappings with which the chair was embellished, concealed the men who carried it; so that to those who viewed him from the area below, his Holiness seemed to sail forward, from the window self-balanced in the air, like a celestial being. The instant he appeared, the music struck up, the bells rung from every church, and the cannon thundered from the castle of St. Angelo in repeated peals. During the intervals, the church of St. Peter's, the palace of the Vatican, and the banks of the Tiber, re-echoed the acclamations of the populace. At length his Holiness arose from his seat, and an immediate and awful silence ensued. The multitude fell upon their knees, with their hands and eyes raised towards his Holiness, as to a benign Deity. After a solemn pause, he pronounced the benediction, with great fervour; elevating his outstretched arms as high as he could; then closing them together, and bringing them back to his breast with a slow motion, as if he had got hold of the blessing, and was drawing it gently from heaven. Finally, he threw his arms open, waving them for some time, as if his intention had been to scatter the benediction with impartiality among the people.

No ceremony can be better calculated for striking the senses, and imposing on the understanding, than this of the Supreme Pontiff giving the blessing from the balcony of St. Peter's. For my own part, if I had not, in my early youth, received impressions highly unfavourable to the chief actor in this magnificent interlude, I should have been in danger of paying him a degree of respect, very inconsistent with the religion in which I was educated.

[1] The Carmen Seculare of Horace was composed on occasion of those celebrated by Augustus in the year of Rome 736.

[2] To this last abridgement I am indebted for having seen the ceremonies and processions on the termination of this sacred year.

LETTER XLIX.

Rome.

In my last, I informed you of my having been seduced almost into idolatry, by the influence of example, and the pomp which surrounded the idol. I must now confess that I have actually bowed the knee to Baal, from mere wantonness. We are told that, to draw near to that Being, who ought to be the only object of worship, with our lips, while our hearts are far from him, is a mockery. Such daring and absurd hypocrisy I shall always avoid: but to have drawn near to *him*, who ought not to be an object of worship, with the lips only, while the heart continued at a distance, I hope will be considered as no more than a venial transgression. In short, I trust, that it will not be looked on as a mortal sin in Protestants to have kissed the Pope's toe. If it should, some of your friends are in a deplorable way, as you shall hear.—It is usual for strangers to be presented to his Holiness, before they leave Rome. The D—— of H——, Mr. K——, and myself, have all been at the Vatican together, upon that important business. Your young acquaintance Jack, who, having now got a commission in the army, considers himself no longer as a boy, desired to accompany us. We went under the auspices of a certain ecclesiastic, who usually attends the English on such occasions.

He very naturally concluded, that it would be most agreeable to us to have the circumstance of kissing the slipper dispensed with. Having had some conversation, therefore, with his Holiness, in his own apartment, while we remained in another room, previous to our introduction; he afterwards returned, and informed us, that the Pontiff, indulgent to the prejudices of the British nation, did not insist on that part of the ceremonial; and therefore a very low bow, on our being presented, was all that would be required of us.

A bow! cried the D—— of H——; I should not have given myself any trouble about the matter, had I suspected that all was to end in a bow. I look on kissing the toe as the only amusing circumstance of the whole; if that is to be omitted, I will not be introduced at all. For if the most ludicrous part is left out, who would wait for the rest of a farce?

This was a thunderstroke to our negociator, who expected thanks, at least, for the honourable terms he had obtained; but who, on the contrary, found himself in the same disagreeable predicament with other negociators, who have met with abuse and reproach from their countrymen, on account of treaties for which they expected universal applause.

The D—— of H—— knew nothing of the treaty which our introducer had just concluded; otherwise he would certainly have prevented the negociation. As I perceived, however, that our ambassador was mortified with the

- 16 -

thoughts that all his labour should prove abortive, I said, that, although he had prevailed with his Holiness to wave that part of the ceremonial, which his Grace thought so entertaining, yet it would unquestionably be still more agreeable to him that the whole should be performed to its utmost extent: this new arrangement, therefore, needed not be an obstruction to our being presented.

The countenance of our Conductor brightened up at this proposal. He immediately ushered us into the presence of the Supreme Pontiff. We all bowed to the ground; the supplest of the company had the happiness to touch the sacred slipper with their lips, and the least agile were within a few inches of that honour. As this was more than had been bargained for, his Holiness seemed agreeably surprised; raised the D——— with a smiling countenance, and conversed with him in an obliging manner, asking the common questions, How long he had been in Italy? Whether he found Rome agreeable? When he intended to set out for Naples?—He said something of the same kind to each of the company; and, after about a quarter of an hour or twenty minutes, we took our leave.

Next day, his Holiness sent his compliments to the D———, with a present of two medals, one of gold, and the other of silver; on both of which the head of the Pontiff is very accurately engraved.

The manner in which the generality of sovereign princes pass their time, is as far from being amusing or agreeable, as one can possibly imagine. Slaves to the tiresome routine of etiquette; martyrs to the oppressive fatigue of pomp; constrained to walk every levee-day around the same dull circle, to gratify the vanity of fifty or a hundred people, by whispering a something or a nothing into the ears of each; obliged to wear a smiling countenance, even when the heart is oppressed with sadness; besieged by the craving faces of those, who are more displeased at what is withheld, than grateful for the favours they have received; surrounded, as he constantly is, by adepts in the art of simulation, all professing the highest possible regard; how shall the puzzled monarch distinguish real from assumed attachment? and what a risk does he run, of placing his confidence where he ought to have directed his indignation! And, to all these inconveniencies, when we add this, that he is precluded from those delightful sensations which spring from disinterested friendship, sweet equality, and the gay, careless enjoyments of social life, we must acknowledge, that all that is brilliant in the condition of a sovereign, is not sufficient to compensate for such restraints, such dangers, and such deprivations.

So far indeed are we from considering that envied condition as enviable, that great part of mankind are more apt to think it insupportable; and are surprised to find, that those unhappy men, whom fate has condemned to suffer the pains of royalty for life, are able to wait with patience for the natural period of their days. For, strange as it may appear, history does not furnish us with an instance, not even in Great Britain itself, of a king, who hanged, or drowned, or put himself to death in any other violent manner, from mere tædium, as other mortals, disgusted with life, are apt to do. I was at a loss to account for such an extraordinary fact, till I recollected that, however void of resources and activity the minds of monarchs may be, they are seldom allowed to rest in repose. The storms to which people in their lofty situation are exposed, occasion such agitations as prevent the stagnating slime of tædium from gathering on their minds. That kings do not commit suicide, therefore, affords only a very slender presumption of the happiness of their condition: although it is a strong proof, that all the hurricanes of life are not so insupportable to the human mind, as that insipid, fearless, hopeless calm, which envelopes men who are devoid of mental enjoyments, and whose senses are palled with satiety. If there is any truth in the above representation of the regal condition, would not you imagine that of all others it would be the most shunned? Would not you imagine that every human being would shrink from it, as from certain misery; and that at least every wise man would say, with the Poet,

I envy none their pageantry and show,

I envy none the gilding of their woe?

Not only every wise man, but every foolish man, will adopt the sentiment, and act accordingly; provided his rank in life removes him from the possibility of ever attaining the objects in question. For what is situated beyond the sphere of our hopes, very seldom excites our desires; but bring the powerful magnets a little nearer, and they attract the human passions with a force which reason and philosophy cannot controul. Placed within their reach, the wise and the foolish grasp with equal eagerness at crowns and sceptres, in spite of all the thorns with which they are surrounded. Their alluring magic seems to have the power of changing the very characters and natures of men. In pursuit of them, the indolent have been excited to the most active exertions, the voluptuous have renounced their darling pleasures; and even those who have long walked in the direct road of integrity, have deviated into all the crooked paths of villany and fraud.

There are passions, whose indulgence is so exceedingly flattering to the natural vanity of men, that they will gratify them, though persuaded that the gratification will be attended by disappointment and misery. The love of power and sovereignty is of this class. It has been a general belief, ever since the kingly office was established among men, that cares and anxiety were the constant attendants of royalty. Yet this general conviction never made a single person decline an opportunity of embarking on this sea of troubles. Every new adventurer flatters himself that he shall be guided by some happy star undiscovered by former navigators; and those who, after trial, have relinquished the voyage—Charles, Christina, Amadeus, and others—when they had quitted the helm, and were safely arrived in port, are said to have languished, all the rest of their lives, for that situation which their own experience taught them was fraught with misery.

Henry the Fourth of England did not arrive at the throne by the natural and direct road. Shakespear puts the following Address to Sleep, into the mouth of this monarch:

——O Sleep! O gentle Sleep!

Nature's soft nurse, how have I frighted thee,

That thou no more wilt weigh my eyelids down,

And steep my senses in forgetfulness?

Why rather, Sleep, liest thou in smoky cribs,

Upon uneasy pallets stretching thee,

And hush'd with busy night-flies to thy slumber;

Than in the perfum'd chambers of the Great,

Under the canopies of costly state

And lull'd with sounds of sweetest melody?

O thou dull God! why ly'st thou with the vile

In loathsome beds; and leav'st the kingly couch?

A watch-case, or a common 'larum bell?

Wilt thou, upon the high and giddy mast,

Seal up the ship-boy's eyes, and rock his brains

In cradle of the rude imperious surge;

And in the visitation of the winds,——

Who take the ruffian billows by the top,

Curling their monstrous heads, and hanging them

With deaf'ning clamours in the slipp'ry shrouds,——

Canst thou, O partial Sleep! give thy repose

To the wet sea-boy in an hour so rude;

And, in the calmest and most stillest night,

With all appliances and means to boot,

Deny it to a King?——

However eager and impatient this Prince may have formerly been to obtain the crown, you would conclude that he was quite cloyed by possession at the time he made this speech; and therefore, at first sight, you would not expect that he should afterwards display any excessive attachment to what gives him so much uneasiness. But Shakespear, who knew the secret wishes, perverse desires, and strange inconsistencies of the human heart, better than man ever knew them, makes this very Henry so tenaciously fond of that which he himself considered as the cause of all his inquietude, that he cannot bear to have the crown one moment out of his sight, but orders it to be placed on his pillow when he lies on his death-bed.

Of all diadems, the Tiara, in my opinion, has the fewest charms; and nothing can afford a stronger proof of the strength and perseverance of man's passion for sovereign power, than our knowledge, that even this ecclesiastical crown is sought after with as much eagerness, perhaps with more, than any other crown in the world, although the candidates are generally in the decline of life, and all of a profession which avows the most perfect contempt of worldly grandeur. This appears the more wonderful when we reflect, that, over and above those sources of weariness and vexation, which the Pope has in common with other sovereigns, he has some which are peculiar to himself.—The tiresome religious functions which he must perform, the ungenial solitude of his meals, the exclusion of the company and conversation of women, restriction from the tenderest and most delightful connexions in life, from the endearments of a parent, and the *open acknowledgment* of his own children; his mind oppressed with the gloomy reflection, that the man for whom he has the least regard, perhaps his greatest enemy, may be his immediate successor; to which is added, the pain of seeing his influence, both spiritual and temporal, declining every day; and the mortification of knowing, that all his ancient lofty pretensions are laughed at by one half of the Roman Catholics, all the Protestants, and totally disregarded by the rest of mankind. I know of nothing which can be put in the other scale to balance all those peculiar disadvantages which his Holiness labours under, unless it is the singular felicity which he lawfully may, and no doubt does enjoy, in the contemplation of his own infallibility.

LETTER L.

In their external deportment, the Italians have a grave solemnity of manner, which is sometimes thought to arise from a natural gloominess of disposition. The French, above all other nations, are apt to impute to melancholy, the sedate serious air which accompanies reflection.

Though in the pulpit, on the theatre, and even in common conversation, the Italians make use of a great deal of action; yet Italian vivacity is different from French; the former proceeds from sensibility, the latter from animal spirits.

The inhabitants of this country have not the brisk look, and elastic trip, which is universal in France; they move rather with a flow composed pace: their spines never having been forced into a straight line, retain the natural bend; and the people of the most finished fashion, as well as the neglected vulgar, seem to prefer the unconstrained attitude of the Antinous, and other antique statues, to the artificial graces of a French dancing-master, or the erect strut of a German soldier. I imagine I perceive a great resemblance between many of the living countenances I see daily, and the features of the ancient busts and statues; which leads me to believe, that there are a greater number of the genuine descendants of the old Romans in Italy, than is generally imagined.

I am often struck with the fine character of countenance to be seen in the streets of Rome. I never saw features more expressive of reflection, sense, and genius; in the very lowest ranks there are countenances which announce minds fit for the highest and most important situations; and we cannot help regretting, that those to whom they belong, have not received an education adequate to the natural abilities we are convinced they possess, and placed where these abilities could be brought into action.

Of all the countries in Europe, Switzerland is that in which the beauties of nature appear in the greatest variety of forms, and on the most magnificent scale; in that country, therefore, the young landscape painter has the best chance of seizing the most sublime ideas: but Italy is the best school for the history painter, not only on account of its being enriched with the works of the greatest masters, and the noblest models of antique sculpture; but also on account of the fine expressive style of the Italian countenance. Here you have few or none of those fair, fat, glistening, unmeaning faces, so common in the more northern parts of Europe. I happened once to sit by a foreigner of my acquaintance at the Opera in the Hay-market, when a certain Nobleman, who at that time was a good deal talked of, entered. I whispered him—"That is Lord ———." "Not surely the famous Lord ———," said he. "Yes," said I, "the very same." "It must be acknowledged then," continued he, "that the noble Earl does infinite honour to those who have had the care of his education." "How so?" rejoined I. "Because," replied the foreigner, "a countenance so completely vacant, strongly indicates a deficiency of natural abilities; the respectable figure he makes in the senate, I therefore presume must be entirely owing to instruction."

Strangers, on their arrival at Rome, form no high idea of the beauty of the Roman women, from the specimens they see in the fashionable circles to which they are first introduced. There are some exceptions; but in general it must be acknowledged, that the present race of women of high rank, are more distinguished by their other ornaments, than by their beauty. Among the citizens, however, and in the lower classes, you frequently meet with the most beautiful countenances. For a brilliant red and white, and all the charms of complexion, no women are equal to the English. If a hundred, or any greater number, of English women were taken at random, and compared with the same number of the wives and daughters of the citizens of Rome, I am convinced, that ninety of the English would be found handsomer than ninety of the Romans; but the probability is, that two or three in the hundred Italians, would have finer countenances than any of the English. English beauty is more remarkable in the country, than in towns; the peasantry of no country in Europe can stand a comparison, in point of looks, with those of England. That race of people have the conveniencies of life in no other country in such perfection; they are no where so well fed, so well defended from the injuries of the seasons; and no where else do they keep themselves so perfectly clean, and free from all the vilifying effects of dirt. The English country girls, taken collectively, are, unquestionably, the handsomest in the world. The female peasants of most other countries, indeed, are so hard worked, so ill fed, so much tanned by the sun, and so dirty, that it is difficult to know whether they have any beauty or not. Yet I have been informed, by some Amateurs, since I came here, that, in spite of all these disadvantages, they sometimes find, among the Italian peasantry, countenances highly interesting, and which they prefer to all the cherry cheeks of Lancashire.

Beauty, doubtless, is infinitely varied; and happily for mankind, their tastes and opinions, on the subject, are equally various. Notwithstanding this variety, however, a style of face, in some measure peculiar to its own inhabitants, has been found to prevail in each different nation of Europe. This peculiar countenance is again greatly varied, and marked with every degree of discrimination between the extremes of beauty and ugliness. I will give you a sketch of the general style of the most beautiful female heads in this country, from which you may judge whether they are to your taste or not.

A great profusion of dark hair, which seems to encroach upon the forehead, rendering it short and narrow; the nose generally either aquiline, or continued in a straight line from the lower part of the brow; a full and short upper lip; by the way, nothing has a worse effect on a countenance, than a large interval between the nose and mouth; the eyes are large, and of a sparkling black. The black eye certainly labours under one disadvantage, which is, that, from the iris and pupil being of the same colour, the contraction and dilatation of the latter is not seen, by which the eye is abridged of half its powers. Yet the Italian eye is wonderfully expressive; some people think it says too much. The complexion, for the most part, is of a clear brown, sometimes fair, but very seldom florid, or of that bright fairness which is common in England and Saxony. It must be owned, that those features which have a fine expression of sentiment and meaning in youth, are more apt, than less expressive faces, to become soon strong and masculine. In England and Germany, the women, a little advanced in life, retain the appearance of youth longer than in Italy.

With countenances so favourable for the pencil, you will naturally imagine, that portrait painting is in the highest perfection here. The reverse, however, of this is true; that branch of the art is in the lowest estimation all over Italy. In palaces, the best furnished with pictures, you seldom see a portrait of the proprietor, or any of his family. A quarter length of the reigning Pope is sometimes the only portrait, of a living person, to be seen in the whole palace. Several of the Roman Princes affect to have a room of state, or audience chamber, in which is a raised seat like a throne, with a canopy over it. In those rooms the effigies of the Pontiffs are hung; they are the work of very inferior artists, and seldom cost above three or four sequins. As soon as his Holiness departs this life, the portrait disappears, and the face of his successor is in due time hung up in its stead. This, you will say, is treating their old sovereign a little unkindly, and paying no very expensive compliment to the new; it is not so œconomical, however, as what was practised by a certain person. I shall not inform you whether he was a Frenchman or an Englishman, but he certainly was a courtier, and professed the highest possible regard for all living monarchs; but considered them as no better than any other piece of clay when dead. He had a full length picture of his own Sovereign in the principal room of his house; on his majesty's death, to save himself the expence of a fresh body, and a new suit of ermine, he employed a painter to brush out the face and periwig, and clap the new King's head on his grandfather's shoulders; which, he declared, were in the most perfect preservation, and fully able to wear out three or four such heads as painters usually give in these degenerate days.

The Italians, in general, very seldom take the trouble of sitting for their pictures. They consider a portrait as a piece of painting, which engages the admiration of nobody but the person it represents, or the painter who drew it. Those who are in circumstances to pay the best artists, generally employ them in some subject more universally interesting, than the representation of human countenances staring out of a piece of canvas.

Pompeio Battoni is the best Italian painter now at Rome. His taste and genius led him to history painting, and his reputation was originally acquired in that line; but by far the greater part of his fortune, whatever that may be, has flowed through a different channel. His chief employment, for many years past, has been painting the portraits of the young English, and other strangers of fortune, who visit Rome. There are artists in England, superior in this, and every other branch of painting, to Battoni. They, like him, are seduced from the free walks of genius, and chained, by interest, to the servile drudgery of copying faces. Beauty is worthy of the most delicate pencil; but, gracious heaven! why should every periwig-pated fellow, without countenance or character, insist on seeing his chubby cheeks on canvas?

"Could you not give a little expression to that countenance?" said a gentleman to an eminent English painter, who showed him a portrait which he had just finished. "I made that attempt already," replied the painter; "but what the picture gained in expression, it lost in likeness; and by the time there was a little common sense in the countenance, nobody knew for whom it was intended. I was obliged, therefore, to make an entire new picture, with the face perfectly like, and perfectly meaningless, as you see it."

Let the colours for ever remain, which record the last fainting efforts of Chatham; the expiring triumph of Wolf; or the indecision of Garrick, equally allured by the two contending Muses! But let them perish and fly from the canvas, which blind self-love spreads for insipidity and ugliness! Why should posterity know, that the first genius of the age, and those whose pencils were formed to speak to the heart, and delineate beauteous Nature, were chiefly employed in copying faces? and many of them, faces that imitate humanity so abominably, that, to use Hamlet's expression, they seem not the genuine work of Nature, but of Nature's journeymen.

To this ridiculous self-love, equally prevalent among the great vulgar and small, some of the best painters in France, Germany, and Great Britain, are obliged for their subsistence. This creates a suspicion, that a taste for the real beauties of painting, is not quite so universal, as a sensibility to their own personal beauties, among the individuals of these countries. And nothing can be a stronger proof of the important light in which men appear in their own eyes, and their small importance in those of others, than the different treatment which the generality of portraits receive, during the life, and after the death, of their constituents. During the first of these periods, they inhabit the finest apartments of the houses to which they belong; they are flattered by the guests, and always viewed with an eye of complacency by the landlord. But, after the commencement of the second, they begin to be neglected; in a short time are ignominiously thrust up to the garret; and, to fill up the measure of their affliction, they finally are thrown out of doors, in the most barbarous manner, without distinction of rank, age, or sex. Those of former times are scattered, like Jews, with their long beards and brown complexions, all over the face of the earth; and, even of the present century, Barons of the most ancient families, armed cap-a-pee, are to be purchased for two or three ducats, in most of the towns of Germany. French Marquises, in full suits of embroidered velvet, may be had at Paris still cheaper; and many worshipful citizens of London are to be seen dangling on the walls of an auction-room, when they are scarce cold in their graves.

LETTER LI.

There are no theatrical entertainments permitted in this city, except during the Carnival; but they are then attended with a degree of ardour unknown in capitals whose inhabitants are under no such restraint. Every kind of amusement, indeed, in this gay season, is followed with the greatest eagerness. The natural gravity of the Roman citizens is changed into a mirthful vivacity; and the serious, sombre city of Rome exceeds Paris itself in sprightliness and gaiety. This spirit seems gradually to augment, from its commencement; and is at its height in the last week of the six which comprehend the Carnival. The citizens then appear in the streets, masked, in the characters of Harlequins, Pantaloons, Punchinellos, and all the fantastic variety of a masquerade. This humour spreads to men, women, and children; descends to the lowest ranks, and becomes universal. Even those who put on no mask, and have no desire to remain unknown, reject their usual clothes, and assume some whimsical dress. The coachmen, who are placed in a more conspicuous point of view than others of the same rank in life, and who are perfectly known by the carriages they drive, generally affect some ridiculous disguise: Many of them chuse a woman's dress, and have their faces painted, and adorned with patches. However dull these fellows may be, when in breeches, they are, in petticoats, considered as the pleasantest men in the world; and excite much laughter in every street in which they appear. I observed to an Italian of my acquaintance, that, considering the staleness of the joke, I was surprised at the mirth it seemed to raise. "When a whole city," answered he, "are resolved to be merry for a week together, it is exceedingly convenient to have a few established jokes ready made; the young laugh at the novelty, and the old from prescription. This metamorphosis of the coachmen is certainly not the most refined kind of wit; however, it is more harmless than the burning of heretics, which formerly was a great source of amusement to our populace."

The street, called the Corso, is the great scene of these masquerades. It is crowded every night with people of all conditions: Those of rank come in coaches, or in open carriages, made on purpose. A kind of civil war is carried on by the company, as they pass each other. The greatest mark of attention you can shew your friends and acquaintance, is, to throw a handful of little white balls, resembling sugar-plums, full in their faces; and, if they are not deficient in politeness, they will instantly return you the compliment. All who wish to make a figure in the Corso, come well supplied in this kind of ammunition.

Sometimes two or three open carriages, on a side, with five or six persons of both sexes in each, draw up opposite to each other, and fight a pitched battle. On these occasions, the combatants are provided with whole bags full of the small shot above mentioned, which they throw at each other, with much apparent fury, till their ammunition is exhausted, and the field of battle is as white as snow.

The peculiar dresses of every nation of the globe, and of every profession, besides all the fantastic characters usual at masquerades, are to be seen on the Corso. Those of Harlequin and Pantaloon are in great vogue among the men. The citizens wives and daughters generally affect the pomp of women of quality; while their brothers, or other relations, appear as train-bearers and attendants. In general, they seem to delight in characters the most remote from their own. Young people assume the long beard, tottering step, and other concomitants of old age; the aged chuse the bib and rattle of childhood; and the women of quality, and women of the town, appear in the characters of country maidens, nuns, and vestal virgins. All endeavour to support the assumed characters, to the best of their ability; but none, in my opinion, succeed so well as those who represent children.

Towards the dusk of the evening, the horse-race takes place. As soon as this is announced, the coaches, cabriolets, triumphal cars, and carriages of every kind, are drawn up, and line the street; leaving a space in the middle for the racers to pass. These are five or six horses, trained on purpose for this diversion; they are drawn up a-breast in the Piazza del Popolo, exactly where the Corso begins. Certain balls, with little sharp spikes, are hung along their sides, which serve to spur them on. As soon as they begin to run, those animals, by their impatience to be gone, shew that they understand what is required of them, and that they take as much pleasure as the spectators in the sport. A broad piece of canvas, spread across the entrance of the street, prevents them from starting too soon: the dropping that canvas is the signal for the race to begin. The horses fly off together, and, without riders, exert themselves to the utmost; impelled by emulation, the shouts of the populace, and the spurs above mentioned. They run the whole length of the Corso; and the proprietor of the victor is rewarded by a certain quantity of fine scarlet or purple cloth, which is always furnished by the Jews.

This diversion, such as it is, seems highly entertaining to the Roman populace; though it appears a mighty foolish business in the eyes of Englishmen. An acquaintance of mine, who had entirely ruined a fine fortune at Newmarket, told me, that Italian horse-races were the most absurd things in the world; that there were not a hundred guineas lost or won during a whole Carnival; and nothing could be a greater proof of the folly of the people, than their spending their time in such a silly manner.

Masking and horse-races are confined to the last eight days; but there are theatrical entertainments, of various kinds, during the whole six weeks of the Carnival. The Serious Opera is most frequented by people of fashion, who generally take boxes for the whole season. The opera, with which this theatre opened, was received with the highest applause, though the music only was new. The Italians do not think it always necessary to compose new words for what is called a new opera; they often satisfy themselves with new music to the affecting dramas of Metastasio. The audience here seem to lend a more profound and continued attention to the music, than at Venice. This is probably owing to the entertainment being a greater rarity in the one city than in the other; for I could perceive that the people of fashion, who came every night, began, after the opera had been repeated several nights, to abate in their attention, to receive visitors in their boxes, and to listen only when some favourite airs were singing: whereas the audience in the pit uniformly preserve the most perfect silence, which is only interrupted by gentle murmurs of pleasure from a few individuals, or an universal burst of applause from the whole assembly. I never saw such genuine marks of satisfaction displayed by any assembly, on any occasion whatever. The sensibility of some of the audience gave me an idea of the power of sounds, which the dulness of my own auditory nerves could never have conveyed to my mind. At certain airs, silent enjoyment was expressed in every countenance; at others, the hands were clasped together, the eyes half shut, and the breath drawn in, with a prolonged sigh, as if the soul was expiring in a torrent of delight. One young woman, in the pit, called out, "O Dio, dove sono! che piacer via caccia l'alma?"

On the first night of the opera, after one of these favourite airs, an universal shout of applause took place, intermingled with demands that the composer of the music should appear. Il Maestro! il Maestro! resounded from every corner of the house. He was present, and led the band of music; he was obliged to stand upon the bench, where he continued, bowing to the spectators, till they were tired of applauding him. One person, in the middle of the pit, whom I had remarked displaying great signs of satisfaction from the beginning of the performance, cried out, "He deserves to be made chief musician to the Virgin, and to lead a choir of angels!" This expression would be thought strong, in any country; but it has peculiar energy here, where it is a popular opinion, that the Virgin Mary is very fond, and an excellent judge, of music. I received this information on Christmas morning, when I was looking at two poor Calabrian pipers doing their utmost to please her, and the Infant in her arms. They played for a full hour to one of her images which stands at the corner of a street. All the other statues of the Virgin, which are placed in the streets, are serenaded in the same manner every Christmas morning. On my enquiring into the meaning of that ceremony, I was told the above-mentioned circumstance of her character, which, though you may have always thought highly probable, perhaps you never before knew for certain. My informer was a pilgrim, who stood listening with great devotion to the pipers. He told me, at the same time, that the Virgin's taste was too refined to have much satisfaction in the performance of those poor Calabrians, which was chiefly intended for the Infant; and he desired me to remark, that the tunes were plain, simple, and such as might naturally be supposed agreeable to the ear of a child of his time of life.

Though the serious opera is in highest estimation, and more regularly attended by people of the first fashion; yet the opera buffas, or burlettas, are not entirely neglected, even by them, and are crowded, every night, by the middle and lower classes. Some admired singers have performed there during the Carnival, and the musical composers have rendered them highly pleasing to the general taste.

The serious and burlesque operas prevail infinitely over the other theatrical entertainments at Rome, in spite of the united efforts of Harlequin, Pantaloon, and Punchinello.

The prohibition of female performers renders the amusement of the Roman theatre very insipid, in the opinion of some unrefined Englishmen of your acquaintance who are here. In my own poor opinion, the natural sweetness of the female voice is ill supplied by the artificial trills of wretched castratos; and the aukward agility of robust sinewy fellows dressed in women's clothes, is a most deplorable substitution for the graceful movements of elegant female dancers. Is not the horrid practice which is encouraged by this manner of supplying the place of female singers, a greater outrage on religion and morality, than can be produced by the evils which their prohibition is intended to prevent? Is it possible to believe, that purity of sentiment will be preserved by producing eunuchs on the stage? I should fear it would have a different effect. At the funeral of Junia, the wife of Cassius, and sister of Brutus, the statues of all the great persons connected with her family by blood or alliance, were carried in procession, except those of her brother and husband. This *deficiency* struck the people more than any part of the procession, and brought the two illustrious Romans into their minds with more force than if their statues had been carried with the others.— Præfulgebant Cassius atque Brutus, says Tacitus, eo ipso, quod effigies eorum non visebantur.

LETTER LII.

I take the first opportunity of informing you of our arrival in this city. Some of the principal objects which occurred on the road, with the sentiments they suggested to my mind, shall form the subject of this letter.

It is almost impossible to go out of the walls of Rome, without being impressed with melancholic ideas. Having left that city by St. John de Lateran's gate, we soon entered a spacious plain, and drove for several miles in sight of sepulchral monuments and the ruins of ancient aqueducts. Sixtus the Fifth repaired one of them, to bring water into that part of Rome where Dioclesian's baths formerly stood: this water is now called *aqua felice*, from Felix, the name of that pontiff, while he was only a Cordelier. Having changed horses at the Torre de Mezzo Via, so called from an old tower near the post-house, we proceeded through a silent, deserted, unwholesome country. We scarce met a passenger between Rome and Marino, a little town about twelve miles from the former, which has its name from Caius Marius, who had a villa there; it now belongs to the Colonna family. While fresh horses were harnessing, we visited two churches, to see two pictures which we had heard commended; the subject of one is as disagreeable, as that of the other is difficult to execute. The connoisseur who directed us to these pieces, told me, that the first, the slaying of St. Bartholomew, by Guercino, is in a great style, finely coloured, and the muscles convulsed with pain in the sweetest manner imaginable; he could have gazed at it for ever. "As for the other," added he "which represents the Trinity, it is natural, well grouped, and easily understood; and that is all that can be said for it."

From Marino, the road runs for several miles over craggy mountains. In ascending Mons Albanus, we were charmed with a fine view of the country towards the sea; Ostia, Antium, the lake Albano, and the fields adjacent. The form and component parts of this mountain plainly shew, that it has formerly been a volcano. The lake of Nemi, which we left to the right, seems, like that of Albano, to have been formed in the cavity of a crater.

We came next to Veletri, an inconsiderable town, situated on a hill. There is one palace here, with spacious gardens, which, when kept in repair, may have been magnificent. The staircase, they assured us, is still worthy of admiration. The inhabitants of Veletri assert, that Augustus was born there. Suetonius says, he was born at Rome. It is certainly of no importance where he was born. Perhaps it would have been better for Rome, and for the world in general, that he never had been born at all. The Veletrians are so fond of emperors, that they claim a connexion even with Tiberius and Caligula, who had villas in their neighbourhood. The ruins of Otho's palace are still to be seen about a mile from this city, at a place called Colle Ottone. Of those four emperors, the last-mentioned was by much the best worth the claiming as a countryman. As for Caligula, he was a mischievous madman. Tiberius seems to have been born with wicked dispositions, which he improved by art. Augustus was naturally wicked, and artificially virtuous; and Otho seems to have been exactly the reverse. Though educated in the most vicious of courts, and the favourite and companion of Nero, he still preserved, in some degree, the original excellence of his character; and, at his death, displayed a magnanimity of sentiment, and nobleness of conduct, of which the highly flattered Augustus was never capable. "Alii diutius imperium tenuerint," says Tacitus; "nemo tam fortiter reliquerit." Convinced that, if he continued the contest with Vitellius, all the horrors of a civil war would be prolonged, he determined to sacrifice his life to the quiet of his country, and to the safety of his friends[3]. "To involve you in fresh calamities," said this generous prince to the officers who offered still to support his cause, "is purchasing life at a price beyond what, in my opinion, is its value. Shall Roman armies be led against each other, and the Roman youth be excited to mutual slaughter, on my account? No! for your safety, and to prevent such evils, I die contented. Let me be no impediment to your treating with the enemy; nor do you any longer oppose my fixed resolution. I complain not of my fate, nor do I accuse any body. To arraign the conduct of gods or men, is natural to those only who wish to live."

Though they are not to be compared in other respects, yet the *death* of Otho may vie with that of Cato; and is one of the strongest instances to be found in history, that a life of effeminacy and voluptuousness does not always eradicate the seeds of virtue and benevolence.

In the middle of the square of Veletri, is a bronze statue of Urban the Eighth. I think they told us it is the workmanship of Bernini.

Descending from that town by a rough road, bordered by vineyards and fruit-trees, we traversed an unsalubrious plain to Sermonetta; between which, and the post-house, called Casa Nuova, a little to the left of the highway, are some vaults and ruins, not greatly worthy of the notice of the mere antiquarian. Yet passengers of a singular cast of mind, who feel themselves as much interested in the transactions recorded in the New Testament, as men of taste are in paintings or heathen antiquities, stop a little here to contemplate the *Tres Tabernæ*, which are said to be the three Taverns mentioned in the Acts of the Apostles, where the Christian brethren from Rome came to meet St. Paul, when he was on his journey to that city. I have seen, however, some Christian travellers, who, without being connoisseurs, were of opinion, that old ruined houses derived little value from the circumstance above mentioned, and who preferred a good modern inn to all the antiquities, sacred or profane, that they met with on their grand tours. Without presuming to blame any set of men for their particular taste, I may venture to say, that a traveller, who loves always to see a well-peopled and well-cultivated country, who insists on good eating every day, and a neat comfortable bed every night, would judge very wisely in never travelling out of England.—I am certain he ought not to travel between Rome and Naples; for on this road, especially the part which runs through the Ecclesiastical State, the traveller's chief entertainment must arise from a less substantial foundation; from the ideas formed in the mind, at sight of places celebrated by favourite authors; from a recollection of the important scenes which have been acted there; and even from the thought of treading the same ground, and viewing the same objects, with certain persons who lived there fifteen hundred or two thousand years ago. Strangers, therefore, who come under the first description, whose senses are far more powerful than their fancy, when they are so ill advised as to come so far from home, generally make this journey in very ill humour, fretting at Italian beds, fuming against Italian cooks, and execrating every poor little Italian flea that they meet with on the road. But he who can put up with indifferent fare cheerfully, whose serenity of temper remains unshaken by the assaults of a flea, and who can draw amusement from the stores of memory and imagination, will find the powers of both wonderfully excited during this journey. Sacred history unites with profane, truth conspires with fable, to afford him entertainment, and render every object interesting.

Proxima Circeæ raduntur littora terræ.

Driving along this road, you have a fine view of Monte Circello, and

——the Æææan bay,

Where Circe dwelt, the daughter of the Day;

Goddess and queen, to whom the powers belong

Of dreadful magic and commanding song.

This abode of the enchantress Circe has been generally described as an island; whereas it is, in reality, a promontory, united to the continent by a neck of land. The adventures of Ulysses and his companions at this place, with all the extraordinary things which Homer has recorded of Circe, must serve to amuse you between Casa Nuova and Piperno; the road affords no other.

At Piperno, anciently Privernum, you quit Circe, for Virgil's Camilla, a lady of a very different character, whose native city this is[4].

Near to Piperno, an abbey, called Fossa Nuova, is situated on the ruins of the little town of Forum Appii, the same of which mention is made in the Acts of the Apostles, and by Horace, in his account of his journey to Brundusium.

——Inde Forum Appi

Differtum nautis, cauponibus atque malignis.

The abbey of Fossa Nuova is said to have made a very valuable acquisition of late, no less than the head of St. Thomas Aquinas. We are told, in the memoirs of that Saint, that he was taken ill as he passed this way, and was carried to this convent, where he died. His body was afterward required by the king of France, and ordered to be carried to Thoulouse; but before the remains of this holy person were removed from the convent, one of the monks, unwilling to allow the whole of such a precious deposite to be carried away, determined to retain the most valuable part, and actually cut off the saint's head, substituting another in its stead, which was carried to Thoulouse, very nicely stitched to the body of the saint. The monk, who was guilty of this pious fraud, hid the true head in the wall of the convent, and died without revealing the secret to any mortal. From that time the supposititious head remained unsuspected at Thoulouse; but as impostures are generally detected sooner or later, the venerable brethren of Fossa Nuova (this happened much about the time that the Cock-lane ghost made such a noise in London) were disturbed with strange knockings and scratchings at a particular part of the wall.—On this noise being frequently repeated, without any visible agent, and the people of the neighbourhood having been often assembled to hear it, the monks at length agreed to pull down part of the wall at the place where the scratching and knocking were always heard. This was no sooner done, than the true head of St. Thomas Aquinas was found as fresh as the day it was cut off;—on the vessel in which it was contained was the following inscription:

Caput divi Thomæ Aquinatis.

And near it a paper, containing a faithful narrative of the whole transaction, signed by the monk who did the deed.

Some people, not making a proper allowance for the difference between a saint's head and their own, say, this cannot possibly be the head of Thomas Aquinas, which must have putrified some centuries ago; they say, the paper is written in a character by much too modern; they say, the monks contrived the whole affair, to give an importance to their convent; they say—but what signifies what they say? In this age of incredulity, some people will say any thing. We next came to Terracina, and here I must finish my letter; in my next I shall carry you to Naples.

[3] Hunc animum, hanc virtutem vestram, ultra periculis objicere, nimis grande vitæ meæ pretium puto. An ego tantum Romanæ pubis, tot egregios exercitus, sterni rursus et republicâ eripi patiar? Este superstites, nec diu moremur; ego incolumitatem vestram, vos constantiam meam. De nemine queror, nam incusare deos vel homines, ejus est, qui vivere velit. TACIT. Hist. lib. ii.

[4]

Hos super advenit Volscâ de gente Camilla,

Agmen agens equitum et florentes ære catervas,

Bellatrix: Non illa colo calathisve Minervæ

Fœmineas assueta manus; sed prœlia virgo

Dura pati, cursuque pedum prævertere ventos.

ÆNEID. lib. vii.

LETTER LIII.

Terracina, formerly called Anxur, was the capital of the warlike Volsci[5]. The principal church was originally a temple of Jupiter, who was supposed to have a partiality for this town, and the country around it. Virgil calls him Jupiter Anxurus. Enumerating the troops who came to support the cause of Turnus, he mentions those who plough the Rutulian hills:

Circeumque jugum; queis Jupiter Anxurus arvis

Præsidet, et viridi gaudens Feronia luco:

Qua saturæ jacet atra palus, &c.

Near this place we fell in again with the Appian Way, and beheld, with astonishment, the depth of rock that has here been cut, to render it more convenient for passengers. This famous road is a paved causeway, begun in the year of Rome 441, by Appius Claudius Cæcus the Censor, and carried all the way from Rome to Capua. It would be superfluous to insist on the substantial manner in which it has been originally made, since it still remains in many places. Though travellers are now obliged to make a circuit by Casa Nuova and Piperno, the Via Appia was originally made in a straight line through the Palude Pontine, or Palus Pomptina, as that vast marsh was anciently called: it is the Ater Palus above mentioned, in the lines quoted from Virgil. That part of the Appian road is now quite impassable, from the augmentation of this noxious marsh, whose exhalations are disagreeable to passengers, and near which it is dangerous to sleep a single night.

Keysler and some others say, that Appius made this road at his own expence. I do not know on what authority they make this assertion; but, whatever their authority may be, the thing is incredible. Could a Roman citizen, at a period when the inhabitants of Rome were not rich, bear an expence which we are surprised that even the State itself could support? Though this famous road has received its name from Appius, I can hardly imagine it was completed by him. The distance from Rome to Capua is above one hundred and thirty miles; a prodigious length for such a road as this to have been made, during the short course of one Censorship; for a man could be Censor only once in his life. This was an office of very great dignity; no person could enjoy it till he had previously been Consul. It was originally held for five years; but, a hundred years before the time of Appius, the term was abridged to eighteen months. He, however, who, as Livy tells us, possessed all the pride and obstinacy of his family, refused to quit the Censorship at the end of that period; and, in spite of all the efforts of the Tribunes, continued three years and a half beyond the term to which the office had been restricted by the Æmilian Law. But even five years is a very short time for so great a work; yet this was not the only work he carried on during his Censorship. "Viam munivit," says the Historian, "et aquam in urbem duxit." The Appian road was carried on, afterwards, from Capua to Brundusium, and was probably completed so far, in the time of Horace; as appears by this verse, in one of his Epistles addressed to Lollius:

Brundusium Numici melius via ducat, an Appi.

Terracina is the last town of the Ecclesiastical, and Fundi the first of the Neapolitan, dominions. This last town stands on a plain, sheltered by hills, which is seldom the case with Italian towns: it probably derives its name from its situation. There is nothing very attractive in this place, now, more than in Horace's time; so we left it as willingly as he did:

Fundos Aufidio Lusco Prætore *libenter* Linquimus.

Continuing our route, partly on the Appian way, we came to Mola di Gaeta, a town built on the ruins of the ancient Formiæ. Horace compliments Ælius Lamia, on his being descended from the first founder of this city:

Auctore ab illo ducis originem,

Qui Formiarum mœnia dicitur,

Princeps.

The same Poet puts the wine, made from the grapes of the Formian hills, on a footing with the Falernian:

————mea nec Falernæ

Temperant vites, neque Formiani

Pocula colles.

Cicero had a villa near this place; and it was on this coast where that great orator was murdered in his litter, as he was endeavouring to make his escape to Greece. The fortress of Gaeta is built on a promontory, about three miles from Mola; but travellers, who have the curiosity to go to the former, generally cross the gulph between the two; and immediately, as the most remarkable thing in the place, they are shewn a great cleft in a rock, and informed that it was miraculously split in this manner at the death of our Saviour. To put this beyond doubt, they shew, at the same time, something like the impression of a man's hand on the rock, of which the following account is given.—A certain person having been told on what occasion the rent took place, struck the palm of his hand on the marble, declaring he could no more believe their story, than that his hand would leave its stamp on the rock; on which, to the terror and confusion of this infidel, the stone yielded like wax, and the impression remains till this day.

Nothing is so injurious to the cause of truth, as attempts to support it by fiction. Many evidences of the justness of this observation occur in the course of a tour through Italy. That mountains were rent at the death of our Saviour, we know from the New Testament; but, as none of them are there particularized, it is presumptuous in others to imagine they can point out what the Evangelists have thought proper to conceal.

This rock, however, is much resorted to by pilgrims; and the Tartanes, and other vessels, often touch there, that the seamen may be provided with little pieces of marble, which they earnestly request may be taken as near the fissure as possible. These they wear constantly in their pockets, in case of shipwreck, from a persuasion, that they are a more certain preservative from drowning, than a cork jacket. Some of these poor people have the misfortune to be drowned, notwithstanding; but the sacred marble loses none of its reputation on that account. Such accidents are always imputed to the weight of the unfortunate person's sins, which have sunk him to the bottom, in spite of all the efforts of the marble to keep him above water; and it is allowed on all hands, that a man so oppressed with iniquity, as to be drowned with a piece of this marble in his pocket, would have sunk much sooner, if, instead of that, he had had nothing to keep him up but a cork jacket.

Strangers are next led to the Castle, and are shewn, with some other curiosities, the skeleton of the famous Bourbon, Constable of France, who was killed in the service of the emperor Charles the Fifth, as he scaled the walls of Rome.

It is remarkable that France, a nation which values itself so much on an affectionate attachment to its princes, and places loyalty at the head of the virtues, should have produced, in the course of the two last centuries, so many illustrious rebels: Bourbon, Coligni, Guise, Turenne, and the Condés; all of them were, at some period of their lives, in arms against their sovereign.

That it is the duty of subjects to preserve their allegiance, however unjustly and tyrannically their prince may conduct himself, is one of the most debasing and absurd doctrines that ever was obtruded on the understanding of mankind. When Francis forgot the services which the gallant Bourbon had rendered him at Mirignan; when, by repeated acts of oppression, he forgot the duty of a king; Bourbon spurned at his allegiance, as a subject. The Spanish nobleman, who declared that he would pull down his house, if Bourbon should be allowed to lodge in it, either never had heard of the injurious treatment which that gallant soldier had received, or he betrayed the sentiments of a slave, and meant to insinuate his own implicit loyalty to the Emperor. Mankind in general have a partiality for princes. The senses are imposed on by the splendour which surrounds them; and the respect due to the office of a king, is naturally converted into an affection for his person: there must therefore be something highly unpopular in the character of the monarch, and highly oppressive in the measures of government, before people can be excited to rebellion. Subjects seldom rise through a desire of attacking, but rather from an impatience of suffering. Where men are under the yoke of feudal lords, who can force them to fight in any cause, it may be otherwise; but when general discontent pervades a free people, and when, in consequence of this, they take arms against their prince, they must have justice on their side. The highest compliment which subjects can pay, and the best service they can render, to a good prince, is, to behave in such a manner, as to convince him that they would rebel against a bad one.

From Mola we were conducted by the Appian way, over the fertile fields washed by the silent Liris:

———Rura quæ Liris quieta

Mordet aqua, taciturnus amnis.

This river bounded Latium. On its banks are still seen some ruins of the ancient Minturnæ. After Manlius Torquatus, in what some will call a phrenzy of virtue, had offered up his son as a sacrifice to military discipline; and his colleague Decius, immediately after, devoted himself in a battle against the Latins; the broken army of that people assembled at Minturnæ, and were a second time defeated by Manlius, and their lands divided by the senate among the citizens of Rome. The first battle was fought near Mount Vesuvius, and the second between Sinuessa and Minturnæ. In the morasses of Minturnæ, Caius Marius, in the seventieth year of his age, was taken, and brought a prisoner to that city, whose magistrates ordered an assassin to put him to death, whom the fierce veteran disarmed with a look. What mortal, says Juvenal, would have been thought more fortunate than Marius, had he breathed out his aspiring soul, surrounded by the captives he had made, his victorious troops, and all the pomp of war, as he descended from his Teutonic chariot, after his triumph over the Cimbri.

———Quid illo cive tulisset

Natura in terris, quid Roma beatius unquam?

Si circumducto captivorum agmine, et omni

Bellorum pompâ, animam exhalâsset opimam,

Cum de Teutonico vellet descendere curru.

Several writers, in their remarks on Italy, observe, that it was on the banks of the Liris that Pyrrhus gained his dear-bought victory over the Romans. They have fallen into this mistake, by confounding the Liris with the Siris, a river in Magna Græcia, near Heraclea; in the neighbourhood of which Pyrrhus defeated the Romans by the means of his elephants.

Leaving Garilagno, which is the modern name of the Liris, we pass the rising ground where the ancient Sinuessa was situated; the city where Horace met his friends Plotius, Varius, and Virgil. The friendly glow with which this admirable painter has adorned their characters, conveys an amiable idea of his own.

————Animæ, quales neque candidiores

Terra tulit; neque queis me sit devinctior alter.

O, qui complexus et gaudia quanta fuerunt!

Nil ego contulerim jucundo sanus amico.

Do you not share in the happiness of such a company? And are you not rejoiced that they happened to meet near the Ager Falernus, where they could have the best Massic and Falernian wines?

New Capua, through which the road from Rome to Naples lies, is a small town of no importance. The ancient city of that name was situated two miles distant from the new. The ruins of the amphitheatre, which are still to be seen, give some idea of the ancient grandeur of that city. Before the amphitheatre of Vespasian was built, there was none in Rome of equal size with this. Old Capua is said, at one period, to have vied in magnificence with Rome and Carthage:

Altera dicta olim Carthago, atque altera Roma,

Nunc prostrata jacet, proprioque sepulta sepulchro.

The army of Hannibal is said to have been conquered by the luxuries of this place; but the judicious Montesquieu observes, that the Carthaginian army, enriched by so many victories, would have found a Capua wherever they had gone. Whether Capua brought on the ruin of Hannibal or not, there can be no doubt that Hannibal occasioned the ruin of Capua.

Having broken their connection with Rome, and formed an alliance with her enemy, the Capuans were, in the course of the war, besieged by the Consuls Fulvius and Appius. Hannibal exerted all his vast abilities for the relief of his new friends; but was not able to bring the Roman army to a battle, or to raise the siege. When every other expedient had failed, he marched directly to Rome, in the hopes of drawing the Roman army after him to defend the capital. A number of alarming events conspired, at this time, to depress the spirit of the Roman Senate. The Proconsul Sempronius Gracchus, who commanded an army in Lucania, had fallen into an ambuscade, and was massacred. The two gallant brothers, the Scipios, who were their generals in Spain, had been defeated and killed; and Hannibal was at their gates. How did the Senate behave at this crisis? Did they spend their time in idle harangues and mutual accusations? Did they throw out reflections against those senators who were against entering into a treaty with the Carthaginians till their army should be withdrawn from Italy? Did they recall their army from Capua? Did they shew any mark of despondence? In this slate of affairs, the Roman Senate sent orders to Appius to continue the siege of Capua; they ordered a reinforcement to their army in Spain; the troops for that service marching out at one gate of Rome, while Hannibal threatened to enter by storm at another. How could such a people fail to become the masters of the world!

The country between Capua and Naples displays a varied scene of lavish fertility, and with great propriety might be named Campania Felix, if the richest and most generous soil, with the mildest and most agreeable climate, were sufficient to render the inhabitants of a country happy.

[5] Anxur fuit quæ nunc Terracinæ sunt; urbs prona in paludes. TIT. LIV. lib. iv.

LETTER LIV.

The day after our arrival at this place, we waited on Sir W——— H———, his Majesty's minister at this court. He had gone early that morning on a hunting party with the King; but the Portuguese ambassador, at L———y H———'s desire, undertook to accompany the D——— on the usual round of visits; Sir W——— was not expected to return for several days, and the laws of etiquette do not allow that important tour to be delayed so long. As we have been continually driving about ever since our arrival, I am already pretty well acquainted with this town, and the environs.

Naples was founded by the Greeks. The charming situation they have chosen, is one proof among thousands, of the fine taste of that ingenious people.

The bay is about thirty miles in circumference, and twelve in diameter; it has been named Crater, from its supposed resemblance to a bowl. This bowl is ornamented with the most beautiful foliage, with vines; with olive, mulberry, and orange trees; with hills, dales, towns, villas, and villages.

At the bottom of the bay of Naples, the town is built in the form of a vast amphitheatre, sloping from the hills towards the sea.

If, from the town, you turn your eyes to the east, you see the rich plains leading to mount Vesuvius, and Portici. If you look to the west, you have the Grotto of Pausilippo, the mountain on which Virgil's tomb is placed, and the fields leading to Puzzoli and the coast of Baia. On the north, are the fertile hills, gradually rising from the shore to the Campagna Felice. On the South, is the bay, confined by the two promontories of Misenum and Minerva, the view being terminated by the islands Procida, Ischia, and Caprea; and as you ascend to the castle of St. Elmo, you have all these objects under your eye at once, with the addition of a great part of the Campagna.

Independent of its happy situation, Naples is a very beautiful city. The style of architecture, it must be confessed, is inferior to what prevails at Rome; but though Naples cannot vie with that city in the number of palaces, or in the grandeur and magnificence of the churches, the private houses in general are better built, and are more uniformly convenient; the streets are broader and better paved. No street in Rome equals in beauty the Strada di Toledo at Naples; and still less can any of them be compared with those beautiful streets which are open to the bay. This is the native country of the Zephyrs; here the excessive heat of the Sun is often tempered with sea breezes, and with gales, wafting the perfumes of the Campagna Felice.

The houses, in general, are five or six stories in height, and flat at the top; on which are placed, numbers of flower vases or fruit trees, in boxes of earth, producing a very gay and agreeable effect.

The fortress of St. Elmo is built on a mountain of the same name. The garrison stationed here, have the entire command of the town, and could lay it in ashes at pleasure. A little lower, on the same mountain, is a convent of Carthusians. The situation of this convent is as advantageous and beautiful as can be imagined; and much expence has been lavished to render the building, the apartments, and the gardens, equal to the situation.

To bestow great sums of money in adorning the retreat of men who have abandoned the world for the express purpose of passing the remainder of their lives in self-denial and mortification, seems to be very ill judged; and might, on some occasions, counteract the design of their retreat. I expressed this sentiment to a Neapolitan lady at Sir W——— H———'s assembly, the evening after I had visited this convent. She said, "that the elegant apartments, the gardens, and all the expensive ornaments I had particularised, could not much impede a system of self-denial; for they soon became insipid to those who had them constantly before their eyes, and proved no compensation for the want of other comforts." "In that case," said I, "the whole expence might have been saved, or bestowed in procuring comforts to others who have made no vows of mortification." "Tolga iddio!" cried the lady, forgetting her former argument, "for none have so good a title to every comfortable and pleasant thing in this world, as those who have renounced it, and placed their affections entirely on the next; instead of depriving these sanctified Carthusians of what they already possess, it would be more meritorious to give them what they have not."

"Give them then, said I, what will afford some satisfaction, instead of the luxuries of sculpture, and paintings and architecture, which, as you say, become so soon insipid; let them have enjoyments of a different kind. Why should their diet be confined to fish and vegetables? Let them enjoy the pleasures of the table without any limitation. And since they are so very meritorious, why is your sex deprived of the happiness of their conversation, and why are they denied the pleasure which the society of women might afford them?"

"Cristo benedetto!" cried the lady, "You do not understand this matter.— Though none deserve the pleasures of this world, but those who think only on the next; yet none can obtain the joys of the next, who indulge in the pleasures of this."

"That is unlucky," said I.

"Unlucky! to be sure it is the most unlucky thing that could have happened, *ecco dove mi doleva*," added the lady.

Though Naples is admirably situated for commerce, and no kingdom produces the necessaries and luxuries of life in greater profusion, yet trade is but in a languishing condition; the best silks come from Lyons, and the best woollen goods from England.

The chief articles manufactured here, at present, are, silk stockings, soap, snuff boxes of tortoise shells, and of the lava of Mount Vesuvius, tables, and ornamental furniture, of marble.

They are thought to embroider here better than even in France; and their macaroni is preferred to that made in any other part of Italy. The Neapolitans excel also in liqueurs and confections; particularly in one kind of confection, which is sold at a very high price, called Diabolonis. This drug, as you will guess from its name, is of a very hot and stimulating nature, and what I should think by no means requisite to Neapolitan constitutions.

The inhabitants of this town are computed at three hundred and fifty thousand. I make no doubt of their amounting to that number; for though Naples is not one third of the size of London, yet many of the streets here are more crowded than the Strand. In London and Paris, the people who fill the streets are mere passengers, hurrying from place to place on business; and when they choose to converge, or to amuse themselves, they resort to the public walks or gardens: at Naples, the citizens have fewer avocations of business to excite their activity; no public walks, or gardens to which they can resort; and are, therefore, more frequently seen sauntering and conversing in the streets, where a great proportion of the poorest sort, for want of habitations, are obliged to spend the night as well as the day. While you sit in your chamber at London, or at Paris, the usual noise you hear from the streets, is that of carriages; but at Naples, where they talk with uncommon vivacity, and where whole streets full of talkers are in continual employment the noise of carriages is completely drowned in the aggregated clack of human voices. In the midst of all this idleness, fewer riots or outrages of any kind happen, than might be expected in a town where the police is far from being strict, and where such multitudes of poor unemployed people meet together every day. This partly proceeds from the national character of the Italians; which, in my opinion, is quiet, submissive, and averse to riot or sedition; and partly to the common people being universally sober, and never inflamed with strong and spirituous liquors, as they are in the northern countries. Iced water and lemonade are among the luxuries of the lowest vulgar; they are carried about in little barrels, and sold in half-penny's worth. The half naked lazzarone is often tempted to spend the small pittance destined for the maintenance of his family, on this bewitching beverage, as the most dissolute of the low people in London spend their wages on gin and brandy; so that the same extravagance which cools the mob of the one city, tends to inflame that of the other to acts of excess and brutality.

There is not, perhaps, a city in the world, with the same number of inhabitants, in which so few contribute to the wealth of the community by useful, or by productive labour, as Naples; but the numbers of priests, monks, fiddlers, lawyers, nobility, footmen, and lazzaronis, surpass all reasonable proportion; the last alone are computed at thirty or forty thousand. If these poor fellows are idle, it is not their own fault; they are continually running about the streets, as we are told of the artificers of China; offering their service, and begging for employment; and are considered, by many, as of more real utility than any of the classes above mentioned.

LETTER LV.

There is an assembly once a week at the house of the British minister; no assembly in Naples is more numerous, or more brilliant, than this. Exclusive of that gentleman's good qualities, and those accomplishments which procure esteem in any situation, he would meet with every mark of regard from the Neapolitan nobles, on account of the high favour in which he stands with their Sovereign. Sir W——'s house is open to strangers of every country who come to Naples properly recommended, as well as to the English; he has a private concert almost every evening. L——y H—— understands music perfectly, and performs in such a manner, as to command the admiration even of the Neapolitans. Sir W——, who is the happiest tempered man in the world, and the easiest amused, performs also, and succeeds perfectly in amusing himself, which is a more valuable attainment than the other.

The Neapolitan nobility are excessively fond of splendour and show. This appears in the brilliancy of their equipages, the number of their attendants, the richness of their dress, and the grandeur of their titles.

I am assured, that the King of Naples counts a hundred persons with the title of Prince, and still a greater number with that of Duke, among his subjects. Six or seven of these have estates, which produce from ten to twelve or thirteen thousand pounds a year; a considerable number have fortunes of about half that value; and the annual revenue of many is not above one or two thousand pounds. With respect to the inferior orders of nobility, they are much poorer; many Counts and Marquisses have not above three or four hundred pounds a year of paternal estate, many still less, and not a few enjoy the title without any estate whatever.

When we consider the magnificence of their entertainments, the splendour of their equipages, and the number of their servants, we are surprised that the richest of them can support such expensive establishments. I dined, soon after our arrival, at the Prince of Franca Villa's; there were about forty people at table; it was meagre day; the dinner consisted entirely of fish and vegetables, and was the most magnificent entertainment I ever saw, comprehending an infinite variety of dishes, a vast profusion of fruit, and the wines of every country in Europe. I dined since at the Prince Iacci's. I shall mention two circumstances, from which you may form an idea of the grandeur of an Italian palace, and the number of domestics which some of the nobility retain. We passed through twelve or thirteen large rooms before we arrived at the dining room; there were thirty-six persons at table, none served but the Prince's domestics, and each guest had a footman behind his chair; other domestics belonging to the Prince remained in the adjacent rooms, and in the hall. We afterwards passed through a considerable number of other rooms in our way to one from which there is a very commanding view.

No estate in England could support such a number of servants, paid and fed as English servants are; but here the wages are very moderate indeed, and the greater number of men servants, belonging to the first families, give their attendance through the day only, and find beds and provisions for themselves. It must be remembered, also, that few of the nobles give entertainments, and those who do not, are said to live very sparingly; so that the whole of their revenue, whatever that may be, is exhausted on articles of show.

As there is no Opera at present, the people of fashion generally pass part of the evening at the Corso, on the sea-shore. This is the great scene of Neapolitan splendour and parade; and, on grand occasions, the magnificence displayed here will strike a stranger very much. The finest carriages are painted, gilt, varnished, and lined, in a richer and more beautiful manner, than has as yet become fashionable either in England or France; they are often drawn by six, and sometimes by eight horses. As the last is the number allotted to his Britannic Majesty when he goes to parliament, some of our countrymen are offended that any individuals whatsoever should presume to drive with the same number.

It is the mode here, to have two running footmen, very gaily dressed, before the carriage, and three or four servants in rich liveries behind; these attendants are generally the handsomest young men that can be procured. The ladies or gentlemen within the coaches, glitter in all the brilliancy of lace, embroidery, and jewels. The Neapolitan carriages, for gala days, are made on purpose, with very large windows, that the spectators may enjoy a full view of the parties within. Nothing can be more showy than the harness of the horses; their heads and manes are ornamented with the rarest plumage, and their tails set off with riband and artificial flowers, in such a graceful manner that you are apt to think they have been adorned by the same hands that dressed the heads of the ladies, and not by common grooms.

After all, you will perhaps imagine the amusement cannot be very great. The carriages follow each other in two lines, moving in opposite directions. The company within smile, and bow, and wave the hand, as they pass and repass their acquaintance; and doubtless imagine, that they are the most important figures in the procession. The horses, however, seem to be quite of a different way of thinking, and to consider themselves as the chief objects of admiration, looking on the livery servants, the volantis, the lords, and the ladies, as their natural suit on all such solemn occasions.

LETTER LVI.

The greatest part of kings, whatever may be thought of them after their death, have the good fortune to be represented, at some period of their lives, generally at the beginning of their reigns, as the greatest and most virtuous of mankind. They are never compared to characters of less dignity than Solomon, Alexander, Cæsar, or Titus; and the comparison usually concludes to the advantage of the living monarch. They differ in this, as in many other particulars, from those of the most distinguished genius and exalted merit among their subjects, That the fame of the latter, if any awaits them, seldom arrives at its meridian till many years after their death; whereas the glory of the former is at its fullest splendour during their lives; and most of them have the satisfaction of hearing all their praises with their own ears. Each particular monarch, taken separately, is, or has been, considered as a star of great lustre; yet any number of them, taken without selection, and placed in the historical galaxy, add little to its brightness, and are often contemplated with disgust. When we have occasion to mention kings in general, the expression certainly does not awaken a recollection of the most amiable or most deserving part of the human species; and tyranny in no country is pushed so far, as to constrain men to speak of them, when we speak in general terms, as if they were. It would revolt the feelings, and rouse the indignation, even of slaves. Full freedom is allowed therefore on this topic; and, under the most arbitrary government, if you chuse to declaim on the imbecility, profligacy, or corruption of human nature, you may draw your illustrations from the kings of any country, provided you take them in groupes, and hint nothing to the detriment of the reigning monarch. But, when we talk of any one living sovereign, we should never allow it to escape from our memory, that he is wise, valiant, generous, and good; and we ought always to have Solomon, Alexander, Cæsar, and Titus, at our elbow, to introduce them apropos when occasion offers. We may have what opinion we please of the whole race of Bourbon; but it would be highly indecent to deny, that the reigning kings of Spain and Naples are very great princes. As I never had the happiness of seeing the father, I can only speak of the son. His Neapolitan Majesty seems to be about the age of six or seven-and-twenty. He is a prince of great activity of body, and a good constitution; he indulges in frequent relaxations from the cares of government and the fatigue of thinking, by hunting and other exercises; and (which ought to give a high idea of his natural talents) he never fails to acquire a very considerable degree of perfection in those things to which he applies. He is very fond, like the King of Prussia, of reviewing his troops, and is perfectly master of the whole mystery of the manual exercise. I have had the honour, oftener than once, of seeing him exercise the different regiments which form the garrison here: he always gave the word of command with his own royal mouth, and with a precision which seemed to astonish the whole Court. This monarch is also a very excellent shot; his uncommon success at this diversion is thought to have roused the jealousy of his Most Catholic Majesty, who also values himself on his skill as a marksman. The correspondence between those two great personages often relates to their favourite amusement.—A gentleman, who came lately from Madrid, told me, that the King, on some occasion, had read a letter which he had just received from his son at Naples, wherein he complained of his bad success on a shooting party, having killed no more than eighty birds in a day: and the Spanish monarch, turning to his courtiers, said, in a plaintive tone of voice, "Mio filio piange di non aver' fatto piu di ottante beccacie in uno giorno, quando mi crederei l'uomo il piu felice del mondo se potesse fare quaranta." All who take a becoming share in the afflictions of a royal bosom, will no doubt join with me, in wishing better success to this good monarch, for the future. Fortunate would it be for mankind, if the happiness of their princes could be purchased at so easy a rate! and thrice fortunate for the generous people of Spain, if the family connexions of their monarch, often at variance with the real interest of that country, should never seduce him into a more ruinous war, than that which he now wages against the beasts of the field and the birds of the air. His Neapolitan Majesty, as I am informed, possesses many other accomplishments; I particularise those only to which I have myself been a witness. No king in Europe is supposed to understand the game of billiards better. I had the pleasure of seeing him strike the most brilliant stroke that perhaps ever was struck by a crowned head. The ball of his antagonist was near one of the middle pockets, and his own in such a situation, that it was absolutely necessary to make it rebound from two different parts of the cushion, before it could pocket the other. A person of less enterprise would have been contented with placing himself in a safe situation, at a small loss, and never have risqued any offensive attempt against the enemy; but the difficulty and danger, instead of intimidating, seemed rather to animate the ambition of this Prince. He summoned all his address; he estimated, with a mathematical eye, the angles at which the ball must fly off; and he struck it with an undaunted mind and a steady hand. It rebounded obliquely, from the opposite side-cushion, to that at the end; from which it moved in a direct line towards the middle pocket, which seemed to stand in gaping expectation to receive it. The hearts of the spectators beat thick as it rolled along; and they shewed, by the contortions of their faces and persons, how much they feared that it should move one hair-breadth in a wrong direction.—I must here interrupt this important narrative, to observe, that, when I talk of contortions, if you form your idea from any thing of that kind which you may have seen around an English billiard-table or bowling-green, you can have no just notion of those which were exhibited on this occasion:

your imagination must triple the force and energy of every English grimace, before it can do justice to the nervous twist of an Italian countenance.—At length the royal ball reached that of the enemy, and with a single blow drove it off the plain. An universal shout of joy, triumph, and applause burst from the beholders; but,

O thoughtless mortals, ever blind to fate,

Too soon dejected, and too soon elate!

the victorious ball, pursuing the enemy too far, shared the same fate, and was buried in the same grave, with the vanquished. This fatal and unforeseen event seemed to make a deep impression on the minds of all who were witnesses to it; and will no doubt be recorded in the annals of the present reign, and quoted by future poets and historians, as a striking instance of the instability of sublunary felicity.

It is imagined that the cabinet of this Court is entirely guided by that of Spain; which, on its part, is thought to be greatly under the influence of French counsels. The manners, as well as the politics, of France, are said to prevail at present at the Court of Madrid. I do not presume to say of what nature the politics of his Neapolitan Majesty are, or whether he is fond of French counsels or not; but no true-born Englishman existing can shew a more perfect contempt of their manners than he does. In domestic life, this Prince is generally allowed to be an easy master, a good-natured husband, a dutiful son, and an indulgent father.

The Queen of Naples is a beautiful woman, and seems to possess the affability, good-humour, and benevolence, which distinguish, in such an amiable manner, the Austrian family.

LETTER LVII.

The hereditary jurisdiction of the nobles over their vassals subsists, both in the kingdom of Naples and Sicily, in the full rigour of the feudal government. The peasants therefore are poor; and it depends entirely on the personal character of the masters, whether their poverty is not the least of their grievances. If the land was leased out to free farmers, whose property was perfectly secure, and the leases of a sufficient length to allow the tenant to reap the fruits of his own improvements, there is no manner of doubt that the estates of the nobility would produce much more. The landlord might have a higher rent paid in money, instead of being collected in kind, which subjects him to the salaries and impositions of a numerous train of stewards; and the tenants, on their parts, would be enabled to live much more comfortably, and to lay up, every year, a small pittance for their families. But the love of domineering is so predominant in the breasts of men who have been accustomed to it from their infancy, that, if the alternative were in their choice, many of them would rather submit to be themselves slaves to the caprices of an absolute prince, than become perfectly independent, on the condition of giving independence to their vassals. There is reason to believe that this ungenerous spirit prevails pretty universally among the nobility all over Europe. The German Barons are more shocked at the idea of their peasants becoming perfectly free, like the farmers of Great Britain, than they are solicitous to limit the power of their princes: And, from the sentiments I have heard expressed by the French, I very much doubt, whether their high nobility would accept of the privileges of English peers, at the expence of that insolent superiority, and those licentious freedoms, with which *they* may, though no English peer can, treat with impunity the citizens and people of inferior rank. We need be the less surprised at this, when we consider that, in some parts of the British empire, where the equable and generous laws of England prevail, those who set the highest value on freedom, who submit to every hardship, and encounter every danger, to secure it to themselves, never have shewn a disposition of extending its blessings, or even alleviating the bondage of that part of the human species, which a sordid and unjustifiable barter has brought into their power.

The Court of Naples has not yet ventured, by one open act of authority, to abolish the immoderate power of the lords over their tenants. But it is believed that the Minister secretly wishes for its destruction; and in cases of flagrant oppression, when complaints are brought before the legal courts, or directly to the King himself, by the peasants against their lord, it is generally remarked that the Minister favours the complainant. Notwithstanding this, the masters have so many opportunities of oppressing, and such various methods of teasing, their vassals, that they generally chuse to bear their wrongs in silence; and perceiving that those who hold their lands immediately from the Crown, are in a much easier situation than themselves; without raising their hopes to perfect freedom, the height of their wishes is to be sheltered, from the vexations of little tyrants, under the unlimited power of one common master. The objects of royal attention, they fondly imagine, are too sublime, and the minds of kings too generous, to stoop to, or even to countenance, in their servants, the minute and unreasonable exertions, which are wrung at present from the hard hands of the exhausted labourer.

Though the Neapolitan nobility still retain the ancient feudal authority over the peasants, yet their personal importance depends, in a great measure, on the favour of the King; who, under pretext of any offence, can confine them to their own estates, or imprison them at pleasure; and who, without any alleged offence, and without going to such extremes, can inflict a punishment, highly sensible to them, by not inviting them to the amusements of the Court, or not receiving them with smiles when they attend on any ordinary occasion. Unless this Prince were so very impolitic as to disgust all the nobility at once, and so unite the whole body against him, he has little to fear from their resentment. Even in case of such an union, as the nobles have lost the affection and attachment of their peasants, what could they do in opposition to a standing army of thirty thousand men, entirely devoted to the Crown? The establishment of standing armies has universally given stability to the power of the prince, and ruined that of the great lords. No nobility in Europe can now be said to inherit political importance, or to act independent of, or in opposition to, the influence of the crown; except the *temporal peers of that part of Great Britain called England.*

As men of high birth are seldom, in this country, called to the management of public affairs, or placed in those situations where great political knowledge is required; and as his Majesty relies on his own talents and experience in war for the direction of the army; neither the civil nor military establishments open any very tempting field for the ambition of the nobles, whose education is usually adapted to the parts in life which they have a probability of acting. Their fortunes and titles descend to them, independent of any effort of their own. All the literary distinctions are beneath their regard; it is therefore not thought expedient to cloud the playful innocence of their childhood, or the amiable gaiety of their youth, with severe study. In some other countries, where a very small portion of literary education is thought becoming for young men of rank, and where even this small portion has been neglected, they sometimes catch a little knowledge of history and mythology, and some useful moral sentiments, from the excellent dramatic pieces that are represented on their theatres. They also sometimes pick up some notion of the different governments in Europe, and a few political ideas, in the course of their travels. But the nobility of this country very seldom travel; and the only dramatic pieces, represented here, are operas; in which music, not sentiment, is the principal thing attended to. In the other theatrical entertainments, Punchinello is the shining character. To this disregard of literature among the nobles, it is owing, that in their body are to be found few tiresome, scholastic pedants, and none of those perturbed spirits, who ruffle the serenity of nations by political alarms, who clog the wheels of government by opposition, who pry into the conduct of ministers, or in any way disturb that total indifference with regard to the public, which prevails all over this kingdom. We are told by a great modern Historian[6], that "force of mind, a sense of personal dignity, gallantry in enterprise, invincible perseverance in execution, contempt of danger and of death, are the characteristic virtues of uncivilised nations." But as the nobles of this country have long been sufficiently civilised, these qualities may in them be supposed to have given place to the arts which embellish a polished age; to gaming, gallantry, music, the parade of equipage, the refinements of dress, and other nameless refinements.

[6] Vide Dr. Robertson's History of the Emperor Charles V. Sect. I.

LETTER LVIII.

Naples.

The citizens of Naples form a society of their own, perfectly distinct from the nobility; and although they are not the most industrious people in the world, yet, having some degree of occupation, and their time being divided between business and pleasure, they probably have more enjoyment than those, who, without internal resources, or opportunities of active exertion, pass their lives in sensual gratifications, and in waiting the returns of appetite around a gaming table. In the most respectable class of citizens, are comprehended the lawyers, of whom there are an incredible number in this town. The most eminent of this profession hold, indeed, a kind of intermediate rank between the nobility and citizens; the rest are on a level with the physicians, the principal merchants, and the artists; none of whom can make great fortunes, however industrious they may be; but a moderate income enables them to support their rank in society, and to enjoy all the conveniences, and many of the luxuries, of life.

England is perhaps the only nation in Europe where some individuals, of every profession, even of the lowest, find it possible to accumulate great fortunes; the effect of this very frequently is, that the son despises the profession of the father, commences gentleman, and dissipates, in a few years, what cost a life to gather. In the principal cities of Germany and Italy, we find, that the ancestors of many of those citizens who are the most eminent in their particular businesses, have transmitted the art to them through several generations. It is natural to imagine, that this will tend to the improvement of the art, or science, or profession, as well as the family fortune; and that the third generation will acquire knowledge from the experience, as well as wealth from the industry, of the former two; whereas, in the cases alluded to above, the wheel of fortune moves differently. A man, by assiduity in a particular business, and by genius, acquires a great fortune and a high reputation; the son throws away the fortune, and ruins his own character by extravagance; and the grandson is obliged to recommence the business, unaided by the wealth or experience of his ancestors. This, however, is pointing out an evil which I should be sorry to see remedied; because it certainly originates in the riches and prosperity of the country in which it exists.

The number of priests, monks, and ecclesiastics of all the various orders that swarm in this city, is prodigious; and the provision appropriated for their use, is as ample, I am assured, that the clergy are in possession of considerably above one-third of the revenue of the whole kingdom, over and above what some particular orders among them acquire by begging for the use of their convents, and what is gotten in legacies by the address and assiduity of the whole. The unproductive wealth, which is lodged in the churches and convents of this city, amounts also to an amazing value. Not to be compared in point of architecture to the churches and convents of Rome, those of Naples surpass them in riches, in the value of their jewels, and in the quantity of silver and golden crucifixes, vessels, and implements of various kinds. I have often heard these estimated at a sum so enormous as to surpass all credibility; and which, as I have no opportunity of ascertaining with any degree of precision, I shall not mention. This wealth, whatever it amounts to, is of as little use to the kingdom, as if it still remained in the mines of Peru; and the greater part of it, surely, affords as little comfort to the clergy and monks as to any other part of the community; for though it belongs to their church, or their convent, yet it can no more be converted to the use of the priests and monks of such churches and convents, than to the tradesmen who inhabit the adjacent streets. For this reason I am a good deal surprised, that no pretext, or subterfuge, has been found, no expedient fallen on, no treaty or convention made, for appropriating part of this at least, to the use of some set of people or other. If the clergy were to lay their hands on it, this might be found fault with by the King; if his Majesty dreamt of taking any part of it for the exigencies of the state, the clergy would undoubtedly raise a clamour; and if both united, the Pope would think he had a right to pronounce his veto; but if all these three powers could come to an understanding, and settle their proportions, I am apt to think a partition might be made as quietly as that of Poland.

Whatever scruples the Neapolitan clergy may have to such a project, they certainly have none to the full enjoyment of their revenues. No class of men can be less disposed to offend Providence by a peevish neglect of the good things which the bounty of heaven has bestowed. Self-denial is a virtue, which I will not say they possess in a smaller degree, but which, I am sure, they affect less than any other ecclesiastics I know; they live very much in society, both with the nobles and citizens. All of them, the monks not excepted, attend the theatre, and seem to join most cordially in other diversions and amusements; the common people are no ways offended at this, or imagine that they ought to live in a more recluse manner. Some of the orders have had the address to make a concern for their temporal interest, and a desire of seeing them live full, and in something of a jolly manner, be regarded by the common people as a proof of zeal for religion. I am informed, that a very considerable diminution in the number of monks has taken place in the kingdom of Naples since the suppression of the Jesuits, and since a liberty of quitting the cowl was granted by the late Pope; but still there is no reason to complain of a deficiency in this order of men. The richest and most commodious convents in Europe, both for male and female votaries, are in this city; the most fertile and beautiful hills of the environs are covered with them; a small part of their revenue is spent in feeding the poor, the monks distributing bread and soup to a certain number every day before the doors of the convents. Some of the friars study physic and surgery, and practise these arts with great applause. Each convent has an apothecary's shop belonging to it, where medicines are delivered gratis to the poor, and sold to those who can afford to pay. On all these accounts the monks in general are greater favourites with the common people than even the secular clergy; all the charity of the friars, however, would not be able to cover their sins, if the stories circulated by their enemies were true,—by which they are represented as the greatest profligates and debauchees in the world. Without giving credit to all that is reported on this subject, as the Neapolitan monks are very well fed, as this climate is not the most favourable to continency (a virtue which in this place is by no means estimated in proportion to its rarity), it is most likely that the inhabitants of the convents, like the inhabitants in general, indulge in certain pleasures with less scruple or restraint than is usual in some other places. Be that as it may, it is certain that they are the most superstitious of mankind; a turn of mind which they communicate with equal zeal and success to a people remarkably ignorant, and remarkably amorous. The seeds of superstition thus zealously sown on such a warm and fertile, though uncultivated, soil, sometimes produce the most extraordinary crops of sensuality and devotion that ever were seen in any country.

The lazzaroni, or black-guards, as has been already observed, form a considerable part of the inhabitants of Naples; and have, on some well-known occasions, had the government for a short time in their own hands. They are computed at above thirty thousand; the greater part of them have no dwelling-houses, but sleep every night under porticos, piazzas, or any kind of shelter they can find. Those of them who have wives and children, live in the suburbs of Naples near Pausilippo, in huts, or in caverns or chambers dug out of that mountain. Some gain a livelihood by fishing, others by carrying burdens to and from the shipping; many walk about the streets ready to run on errands, or to perform any labour in their power for a very small recompence. As they do not meet with constant employment, their wages are not sufficient for their maintenance; the soup and bread distributed at the door of the convents supply the deficiency. The lazzaroni are generally represented as a lazy, licentious, and turbulent set of people; what I have observed gives me a very different idea of their character. Their idleness is evidently the effect of necessity, not of choice; they are always ready to perform any work, however laborious, for a very reasonable gratification. It must proceed from the fault of Government, when such a number of stout active citizens remain unemployed; and so far are they from being licentious and turbulent, that I cannot help thinking they are by much too tame and submissive. Though the inhabitants of the Italian cities were the first who shook off the feudal yoke, and though in Naples they have long enjoyed the privilege of municipal jurisdiction, yet the external splendour of the nobles, and the authority they still exercise over the peasants, impose upon the minds of the lazzaroni; and however bold and resentful they may be of injuries offered by others, they bear the insolence of the nobility as passively as peasants fixed to the soil. A coxcomb of a volanti tricked out in his fantastical dress, or any of the liveried slaves of the great, make no ceremony of treating these poor fellows with all the insolence and insensibility natural to their matters; and for no visible reason, but because he is dressed in lace, and the others in rags. Instead of calling to them to make way, when the noise in the streets prevents the common people from hearing the approach of the carriage, a stroke across the shoulders with the cane of the running footman, is the usual warning they receive. Nothing animates this people to insurrection, but some very pressing and very universal cause; such as a scarcity of bread: every other grievance they bear as if it were their charter. When we consider thirty thousand human creatures without beds or habitations, wandering almost naked in search of food through the streets of a well built city; when we think of the opportunities they have of being together, of comparing their own destitute situation with the affluence of others, one cannot help being astonished at their patience.

Let the prince be distinguished by splendour and magnificence; let the great and the rich have their luxuries; but, in the name of humanity, let the poor, who are willing to labour, have food in abundance to satisfy the cravings of nature, and raiment to defend them from the inclemencies of the weather!

If their governors, whether from weakness or neglect, do not supply them with these, they certainly have a right to help themselves.—Every law of equity and common sense will justify them, in revolting against such governors, and in satisfying their own wants from the superfluities of lazy luxury.

LETTER LIX.

I have made several visits to the museum at Portici, principally, as you may believe, to view the antiquities dug out of Herculaneum and Pompeia. The work publishing by Government, ornamented with engravings of the chief articles of this curious collection, will, in all probability, be continued for many years, as new articles worthy of the sculptor's art are daily discovered, and as a vast mine of curiosities is supposed to be concealed in the unopened streets of Pompeia. Among the ancient paintings, those which ornamented the theatre of Herculaneum are more elegant than any that have hitherto been found at Pompeia. All those paintings were executed upon the stucco which lined the walls; they have been sawed off with great labour and address, and are now preserved in glass cases; the colours, we are told, were much brighter before they were drawn out of their subterraneous abode, and exposed to the open air; they are, however, still wonderfully lively: the subjects are understood at the first glance by those who are acquainted with the Grecian history and mythology. There is a Chiron teaching Achilles to play on the lyre, Ariadne deserted, the Judgment of Paris, some Bacchantes and Fauns; the largest piece represents Theseus's victory over the Minotaur. It consists of seven or eight figures very well grouped, but a Frieze, with a dancing woman, on a black ground, not above ten inches long, is thought the best.

We ought not, however, to judge of the progress which the ancients had made in the art of painting, by the degree of perfection which appears in those pictures. It is not probable that the best paintings of ancient Greece or Italy were at Herculaneum; and, if it could be ascertained that some of the productions of the best matters were there, it would not follow that those which have been discovered are of that class. If a stranger were to enter at random a few houses in London, and see some tolerably good pictures there, he could not with propriety conclude that the best of them were the very best in London. The paintings brought from Herculaneum are perfect proofs that the ancients had made that progress in the art, which those pictures indicate; but do not form even a presumption, that they had not made a much greater. It is almost demonstrable that these paintings are not of their best. The same school which formed the sculptor to correctness, would form the painter to equal correctness in his drawings, however deficient he might be in all the other parts of his art. Their best statues are correct in their proportions, and elegant in their forms: These paintings are not correct in their proportions, and are comparatively inelegant in their forms.

Among the statues, the drunken Faun and the Mercury are the best. There are some fine bronze busts; the intaglios and cameos, which hitherto have been found either in Herculaneum or Pompeia, are reckoned but indifferent.

The elegance of form, with the admirable workmanship, of the ornamental furniture and domestic utensils, in silver and other metals; the variety and beauty of the lamps, tripods, and vases; sufficiently testify, if there were no other proofs, the fertile imagination and exquisite execution of the ancient artists. And, had their own poets and historians been quite silent concerning the Roman refinements in the art of cookery, and the luxury of their tables; the prodigious variety of culinary instruments, the moulds for jellies, for confections, and pastry, which are collected in this museum, would afford a strong presumption that the great men of our own days have a nearer resemblance to those ancient conquerors of the world, than is generally imagined.

Many of the ancient manuscripts found at Herculaneum have been carried to Madrid; but a great number still remain at Portici. Great pains have been bestowed, and much ingenuity displayed, in separating and unrolling the sheets, without destroying the writing. This has succeeded in a certain degree; though, in spite of all the skill and attention of those who are employed in this very delicate work, the copiers are obliged to leave many blanks where the letters are obliterated. The manuscripts hitherto unrolled and copied, are in the Greek language, and not of a very important nature. As the unrolling those papers must take up a great deal of time, and requires infinite address, it is to be wished that his Neapolitan Majesty would send one at least to every university in Europe, that the abilities of the most ingenious men of every country might be exercised on a subject so universally interesting. The method which should be found to succeed best, might be immediately made known, and applied to the unfolding of the remaining manuscripts. The probability of recovering those works, whose loss the learned have so long lamented, would by this means be greatly increased.

Herculaneum and Pompeia were destroyed by the same eruption of Mount Vesuvius, about seventeen hundred years ago. The former was a town of much more magnificence than the other; but it is infinitely more difficult to be cleared of the matter which covers it. Sir William Hamilton, in his accurate and judicious observations on Mount Vesuvius, asserts, that there are evident marks that the matter of six eruptions has taken its course over this devoted town, since the great explosion which involved it in the same fate with Pompeia. These different eruptions have all happened at considerable distances of time from each other. This appears by the layers of good soil which are found between them. But the matter which immediately covers the town, and with which the theatre, and all the houses hitherto examined, were found filled, is not lava, but a sort of soft stone, composed of pumice and ashes, intermixed with earth. This has saved the pictures, manuscripts, busts, utensils, and other antiquities, which have been recovered out of Herculaneum, from utter destruction. For if any of the six succeeding eruptions had happened previous to this, and the red-hot liquid lava, of which they consisted, had flowed into the open city, it would have filled every street, scorched up every combustible substance with intense heat, involving the houses, and all they contained, in one solid rock of lava, undistinguishable, and for ever inseparable, from it. The eruption, which buried the city in cinders, earth, and ashes, has in some measure preserved it from the more destructive effects of the fiery torrents which have overwhelmed it since.

When we consider that the intervals between those eruptions were sufficiently long to allow a soil to be formed upon the hardened lava of each; that a new city has been actually built on the lava of the last eruption; and that the ancient city is from seventy to one hundred feet below the present surface of the earth; we must acknowledge it more surprising that any, than that so few, of its ornaments have been recovered. At the beginning of the present century, any body would have imagined that the busts, statues and pictures of Herculaneum had not a much better chance, than the persons they represent, of appearing again, within a few years, upon the surface of this globe.

The case is different with regard to Pompeia. Though it was not discovered till about twenty-five years ago, which is forty years almost after the discovery of Herculaneum, yet the probability was greatly in favour of its being discovered sooner, for Pompeia has felt the effects of a single eruption only; it is not buried above twelve feet below the surface of the ground, and the earth, ashes, cinders, and pumice-stones, with which it is covered, are so light, and so little tenacious, that they might be removed with no great difficulty. If the attention of his Neapolitan Majesty were not engrossed with more important concerns, he might have the whole town uncovered in a very short space of time; half the lazzaroni of Naples could complete the business in one year. Hitherto only one street and a few detached buildings are cleared; the street is well paved with the same kind of stone of which the ancient roads are made, narrow causeways are raised a foot and an half on each side for the conveniency of foot passengers. The street itself, to my recollection, is not so broad as the narrowest part of the Strand, and is supposed to have been inhabited by tradespeople. The traces of wheels of carriages are to be seen on the pavement; the distance between the traces is less than that between the wheels of a modern post-chaise. I remarked this the more as, on my first viewing the street, I doubted whether there was room for two modern coaches to pass each other. I plainly saw there was sufficient room for two of the ancient chariots, whose wheels were of no greater distance than between the traces on the pavement. The houses are small, and in a very different style from the modern Italian houses; for the former give an idea of neatness and conveniency. The stucco on the walls is hard as marble, smooth and beautiful. Some of the rooms are ornamented with paintings, mostly single figures, representing some animal; they are tolerably well executed, and on a little water being thrown on them, the colours appear surprisingly fresh.

Most of the houses are built on the same plan, and have one small room from the passage, which is conjectured to have been the shop, with a window to the street, and a place which seems to have been contrived for shewing the goods to the greatest advantage. The nature of the traffic carried on at one particular house, is indicated by a figure in alto relievo of a very expressive kind, immediately above the door.

It is to be wished they would cover one of the best houses with a roof, as nearly resembling that which originally belonged to it as they could imagine, with a complete assortment of the antique furniture of the kitchen and each particular room. Such a house fitted up with accuracy and judgment, with all its utensils and ornaments properly arranged, would be an object of universal curiosity, and would swell the heart of the antiquarian with veneration and delight. Only imagine, my dear Sir, what those gentlemen must feel, when they see the venerable habitations of the ancients in their present mournful condition, neglected, despised, abandoned to the peltings of rain, and all the injuries of the weather! those precious walls, which, were it possible to transport them to the various countries of the world, would be bought with avidity, and placed in the gardens of Princes! How must the bosoms of all true virtuosos glow with indignation, when they behold the mansions of the ancient Romans stripped of their ornaments, dishonoured, and exposed, like a parcel of ragged galley slaves, in the most indecent manner, with hardly any covering to their nakedness; while a little paltry brick house, coming the Lord knows how, from a country which men of taste have always despised, has been received with hospitality, dressed in a fine coat of the richest marble, adorned with jewels and precious stones, and treated with every mark of honourable distinction!

In another part of the town of Pompeia, there is a rectangular building, with a colonade, towards the court, something in the style of the Royal Exchange at London, but smaller. This has every appearance of a barrack and guard room; the pillars are of brick, covered with shining stucco, elegantly fluted; the scrawlings and drawings still visible on the walls, are such as we might naturally expect on the walls of a guard room, where soldiers are the designers, and swords the engraving tools. They consist of gladiators fighting, some with each other, some with wild beasts; the games of the circus, as chariot races, wrestling, and the like; a few figures in caricatura, designed probably by some of the soldiers, in ridicule of their companions, or perhaps of their officers; and there are abundance of names inscribed on various parts of the wall, according to the universal custom of the humblest candidates for fame in all ages and countries. It may be safely asserted, that none of those who have endeavoured to transmit their names to posterity in this manner, have succeeded so well as the soldiers of the garrison of Pompeia.

At a considerable distance from the barrack, is a building, known by the inscription upon it, for a temple of the goddess Isis; there is nothing very magnificent in its appearance; the pillars are of brick stuccoed like those of the guard room. The best paintings, hitherto found at Pompeia, are those of this temple; they have been cut out of the walls and removed to Portici. It was absolutely necessary to do this with the pictures at Herculaneum, because *there* they could not be seen without the help of torches; but *here*, where they could be seen by the light of the Sun, they would, in my humble opinion, have appeared to more advantage, and have had a better effect in the identical situation in which they were placed by the ancient artist. A few still remain, particularly one, which is considered by travellers as a great curiosity; it is a small view of a villa, with the gardens belonging to it.

There is one house or villa without the walls, on a much larger scale than any of the others. In a large cellar, or vaulted gallery, belonging to this house, there are a number of amphoræ, or earthen vessels, arranged along the walls; most of them filled with a kind of red substance, supposed to have been wine. This cellar is sunk about two-thirds below the surface of the ground, and is lighted by small narrow windows. I have called it gallery, because it is about twelve feet in width, and is the whole length of two adjoining sides of the square which the villa forms. It was used not only as a repository for wine, but also as a cool retreat for the family during excessive hot weather. Some of this unfortunate family sought shelter in this place from the destructive shower which overwhelmed the town. Eight skeletons, four being those of children, were found here; where they must have met a more cruel and lingering death, than that which they shunned. In one room, the body of a man was found; with an ax in the hand; it is probable he had been endeavouring to cut a passage into the open air; he had broken and pierced the wall, but had expired before he could clear away the surrounding rubbish. Few skeletons were found in the streets, but a considerable number in the houses. Before the decisive shower fell, which smothered the inhabitants of this ill fated city, perhaps such quantities of ashes and cinders were occasionally falling, as frightened, and obliged them to keep within doors.

It is impossible to view those skeletons, and reflect on this dreadful catastrophe, without horror and compassion. We cannot think of the inhabitants of a whole town being destroyed at once, without imagining that their fate has been uncommonly severe. But are not the inhabitants of all the towns then existing, of whom we think without any emotion of pity, as completely dead as those of Pompeia? And could we take them one by one, and consider the nature of their deaths, and the circumstances attending that of each individual; some destroyed by painful bodily diseases, some by the torture of the executioner, some bowed to the grave by the weight of accumulated sorrow, and the slow anguish of a broken heart, after having suffered the pangs of dissolution, over and over again, in the death of those they loved, after having beheld the dying agonies of their children; could all this, I say, be appraised, calculated, and compared, the balance of suffering might not be found with the inhabitants of Pompeia, but rather with those of the contemporary cities, who, perhaps at that time, as we do now, lamented its severe fate.

LETTER LX.

As I sauntered along the Strada Nuova lately, I perceived a groupe of people listening, with much attention, to a person who harangued them in a raised, solemn voice, and with great gesticulation. I immediately made one of the auditory, which increased every moment; men, women, and children bringing seats from the neighbouring houses, on which they placed themselves around the orator. He repeated stanzas from Ariosto, in a pompous, recitativo cadence, peculiar to the natives of Italy; and he had a book in his hand, to assist his memory when it failed. He made occasional commentaries in prose, by way of bringing the Poet's expression nearer to the level of his hearers' capacities. His cloak hung loose from one shoulder; his right arm was disengaged, for the purposes of oratory. Sometimes he waved it with a slow, smooth motion, which accorded with the cadence of the verses; sometimes he pressed it to his breast, to give energy to the pathetic sentiments of the Poet. Now he gathered the hanging folds of the right side of his cloak, and held them gracefully up, in imitation of a Roman senator; and anon he swung them across his left shoulder, like a citizen of Naples. He humoured the stanza by his voice, which he could modulate to the key of any passion, from the boisterous bursts of rage, to the soft notes of pity or love. But, when he came to describe the exploits of Orlando, he trusted neither to the powers of his own voice, nor the Poet's genius; but, throwing off his cloak, and grasping his cane, he assumed the warlike attitude and stern countenance of that hero; representing, by the most animated action, how he drove his spear through the bodies of six of his enemies at once; the point at the same time killing a seventh, who would also have remained transfixed with his companions, if the spear could have held more than six men of an ordinary size upon it at a time.

Il Cavalier d' Anglante ove pui spesse

Vide le genti e l'arme, abbasso l'asta,

Ed uno in quella, e poscia un altro messe

E un altro, e un altro, che sembrar di pasta,

E fino a sei ve n'infilzò, e li resse

Tutti una lancia; e perche' ella non basta

A piu Capir, lasciò il settimo fuore

Ferito si che di quel colpo muore.

This stanza our declaimer had no occasion to comment upon, as Ariosto has thought fit to illustrate it in a manner which seemed highly to the taste of this audience. For, in the verse immediately following, Orlando is compared to a man killing frogs in marshy ground, with a bow and arrow made for that purpose; an amusement very common in Italy, and still more so in France.

Non altrimente nell' estrema arena

Veggiam le rane de' canali e fosse

Dal cauto arcier ne i fianchi, e nella schiena

L'una vicina all' altera esser percosse,

Ne dalla freccia, fin che tutta piena

Non sia da un capo all' altero esser rimosse.

I must however do this audience the justice to acknowledge, that they seemed to feel the pathetic and sublime, as well as the ludicrous, parts of the ancient Bard.

This practice of rehearsing the verses of Ariosto, Tasso, and other poets, in the street, I have not observed in any other town of Italy; and I am told it is less common here than it was formerly. I remember indeed, at Venice, to have frequently seen mountebanks, who gained their livelihood by amusing the populace at St. Mark's Place, with wonderful and romantic stories in prose.—"Listen, Gentlemen," said one of them; "let me crave your attention, ye beautiful and virtuous ladies; I have something equally affecting and wonderful to tell you; a strange and stupendous adventure, which happened to a gallant knight."—Perceiving that this did not sufficiently interest the hearers, he exalted his voice, calling out that his Knight was uno Cavalliero Cristiano. The audience seemed still a little fluctuating. He raised his voice a note higher, telling them that this Christian Knight was one of their own victorious countrymen, "un' Eroe Veneziano." This fixed them; and he proceeded to relate how the Knight, going to join the Christian army, which was on its march to recover the Sepulchre of Christ from the hands of the Infidels, lost his way in a vast wood, and wandered at length to a castle, in which a lady of transcendent beauty was kept prisoner by a gigantic Saracen, who, having failed in all his endeavours to gain the heart of this peerless damsel, resolved to gratify his passion by force; and had actually begun the horrid attempt, when the shrieks of this chaste maiden reached the ears of the Venetian hero; who, ever ready to relieve virgins in distress, rushed into the apartment from whence the cries issued. The brutal ravisher, alarmed at the noise, quits the struggling lady, at the very instant when her strength began to fail; draws his flaming sword; and a dreadful combat begins between him and the Christian Knight, who performs miracles of courage and address in resisting the blows of this mighty giant; till, his foot unfortunately slipping in the blood which flowed on the pavement, he fell at the feet of the Saracen; who, immediately seizing the advantage which chance gave him, raised his sword with all his might, and—Here the orator's hat flew to the ground, open to receive the contributions of the listeners; and he continued repeating, "raised his sword over the head of the Christian Knight"—"raised his bloody, murderous brand, to destroy your noble, valiant countryman."—But he proceeded no farther in his narrative, till all who seemed interested in it had thrown something into the hat. He then pocketed the money with great gravity, and went on to inform them, that, at this critical moment, the Lady, seeing the danger which threatened her deliverer, redoubled her prayers to the Blessed Mary, who, a virgin herself, is peculiarly attentive and propitious to the prayers of virgins. Just as the Saracen's sword was descending on the head of the Venetian, a large bee flew, quick as thought, in at the window, stung the former very smartly on the left temple, diverted the blow, and gave the Christian Knight time to recover himself. The fight then recommenced with fresh fury; but, after the Virgin Mary had taken such a decided part, you may believe it was no match. The Infidel soon fell dead at the feet of the Believer. But who do you think this beauteous maiden was, on whose account the combat had begun? Why no other than the sister of the Venetian Hero.—This young lady had been stolen from her father's house, while she was yet a child, by an Armenian merchant, who dealt in no other goods than women. He concealed the child till he found means to carry her to Egypt; where he kept her in bondage, with other young girls, till the age of fifteen, and then sold her to the Saracen. I do not exactly remember whether the recognition between the brother and sister was made out by means of a mole on the young lady's neck, or by a bracelet on her arm, which, with some other of her mother's jewels, happened to be in her pocket when she was stolen; but, in whatever manner this came about, there was the greatest joy on the happy occasion; and the lady joined the army with her brother, and one of the Christian commanders fell in love with her, and their nuptials were solemnized at Jerusalem; and they returned to Venice, and had a very numerous family of the finest children you ever beheld.

At Rome, those street-orators sometimes entertain their audience with interesting passages of real history. I remember having heard one, in particular, give a full and true account how the bloody heathen emperor Nero set fire to the city of Rome, and sat at a window of his golden palace, playing on a harp, while the town was in flames. After which the Historian proceeded to relate, how this unnatural emperor murdered his own mother; and he concluded by giving the audience the satisfaction of hearing a particular detail of all the ignominious circumstances attending the murderer's own death.

This business of street-oratory, while it amuses the populace, and keeps them from less innocent and more expensive pastimes, gives them at the same time some general ideas of history. Street-orators, therefore, are a more useful set of men than another class, of which there are numbers at Rome, who entertain companies with extemporaneous verses on any given subject. The last are called Improuvisatoris; and some people admire these performances greatly. For my own part, I am too poor a judge of the Italian language either to admire or condemn them; but, from the nature of the thing, I should imagine they are but indifferent. It is said, that the Italian is peculiarly calculated for poetry, and that verses may be made with more facility in this than in any other language. It may be more easy to find smooth lines, and make them terminate in rhime in Italian, than in any language; but to compose verses with all the qualities essential to good poetry, I imagine leisure and long reflection are requisite. Indeed I understand, from those who are judges, that those extempore compositions of the Improuvisatori are in general but mean productions, consisting of a few fulsome compliments to the company, and some common-place observations, put into rhime, on the subject proposed. There is, however, a lady of an amiable character, Signora Corilla, whose extempore productions, which she repeats in the most graceful manner, are admired by people of real taste. While we were at Rome, this lady made an appearance one evening, at the assembly of the Arcadi, which charmed a very numerous company; and of which our friend Mr. R— y has given me such an account, as makes me regret that I was not present. After much entreaty, a subject being given, she began, accompanied by two violins, and sung her unpremeditated strains with great variety of thought and elegance of language. The whole of her performance lasted above an hour, with three or four pauses, of about five minutes each, which seemed necessary, more that she might recover her strength and voice, than for recollection; for that gentleman said, that nothing could have more the air of inspiration, or what we are told of the Pythian Prophetess. At her first setting out, her manner was sedate, or rather cold; but gradually becoming animated, her voice rose, her eyes sparkled, and the rapidity and beauty of her expressions and ideas seemed supernatural. She at last called on another member of the society to sing alternately with her, which he complied with; but Mr. R——y thought, though they were *Arcades ambo*, they were by no means *cantare pares*.

Naples is celebrated for the finest opera in Europe. This however happens not to be the season of performing; but the common people enjoy *their* operas at all seasons. Little concerts of vocal and instrumental music are heard every evening in the Strada Nuova, the Chiaca, the Strada di Toledo, and other streets; and young men and women are seen dancing to the music of ambulatory performers all along this delightful bay. To a mere spectator, the amusements of the common people afford more delight, than those of the great; because they seem to be more enjoyed by the one class, than by the other. This is the case every where, except in France; where the high appear as happy as those of middle rank, and the rich are very near as merry as the poor. But, in most other countries, the people of great rank and fortune, though they flock to every kind of entertainment, from not knowing what to do with themselves, yet seem to enjoy them less than those of inferior rank and fortune.

The English particularly are said to be in this predicament. This may be true in some degree; though I imagine there is more appearance than reality in it; owing to an absurd affectation of indifference, or what the French call *nonchalance*, which has prevailed of late years. A few insipid characters in high life, whose internal vacancy leads them to seek amusement in public places, and whose insensibility prevents them from finding it, have probably brought this appearance of a want of all enjoyment into fashion. Those who wish to be thought of what is called the *ton*, imitate the mawkish insipidity of their superiors in rank, and imagine it distinguishes them from the vulgar, to suppress all the natural expressions of pity, joy, or admiration, and to seem, upon all occasions, in a state of complete apathy. Those amiable creatures frequent public places, that it may be said of them, *They are not as other men are.* You will see them occasionally at the playhouse, placed in the boxes, like so many busts, with unchanging features; and, while the rest of the audience yield to the emotions excited by the poet and the actors, those men of the *ton* preserve the most dignified serenity of countenance; and, except that they from time to time pronounce the words *Pshaw!* and *Stuff!*—one would think them the express representatives of the Pagan gods, who *have eyes but do not see, and ears but do not hear.*

I know not what may be the case at the opera; but I can assure you there are none of those busts among the auditories which the street-performers at Naples gather around them. I saw very lately a large cluster of men, women, and children, entertained to the highest degree, and to all appearance made exceedingly happy, by a poor fellow with a mask on his face, and a guitar in his hands. He assembled his audience by the songs he sung to the music of his instrument, and by a thousand merry stories he told them with infinite drollery. This assembly was in an open place, facing the bay, and near the palace. The old women sat listening, with their distaffs, spinning a kind of coarse flax, and wetting the thread with their spittle; their grandchildren sprawled at their feet, amused with the twirling of the spindle. The men and their wives, the youths and their mistresses, sat in a circle, with their eyes fixed on the musician, who kept them laughing for a great part of the evening with his stories, which he enlivened occasionally with tunes upon the guitar. At length, when the company was most numerous, and at the highest pitch of good humour, he suddenly pulled off his mask, laid down his guitar, and opened a little box which stood before him, and addressed the audience in the following words, as literally as I can translate them:—"Ladies and gentlemen, there is a time for all things; we have had enough of jesting; innocent mirth is excellent for the health of the body, but other things are requisite for the health of the soul. I will now, with your permission, my honourable masters and mistresses, entertain you with something serious, and of infinitely greater importance; something for which all of you will have reason to bless me as long as you live." Here he shook out of a bag a great number of little leaden crucifixes.—"I am just come from the Holy House of Loretto, my fellow christians," continued he, "on purpose to furnish you with those jewels, more precious than all the gold of Peru, and all the pearls of the ocean. Now, my beloved brethren and sisters, you are afraid that I shall demand a price for those sacred crosses, far above your abilities, and something correspondent with their value, by way of indemnification for the fatigue and expence of the long journey which I have made on your account, all the way from the habitation of the Blessed Virgin to this thrice renowned city of Naples, the riches and liberality of whose inhabitants are celebrated all over the globe. No, my generous Neapolitans; I do not wish to take the advantage of your pious and liberal dispositions, I will not ask for those invaluable crucifixes (all of which, let me inform you, have touched the soot of the holy image of the Blessed Virgin, which was formed by the hands of St. Luke; and, moreover, each of them has been shaken in the Santissima Scodella, the sacred porringer in which the Virgin made the pap for the infant Jesus); I will not, I say, ask an ounce of gold, no not even a crown of silver; my regard for you is such, that I shall let you have them for a penny a piece."

You must acknowledge, my friend, that this morsel of eloquence was a very great pennyworth; and when we recollect the sums that some of our acquaintance receive for their oratory, though they never could produce so pathetic a specimen, you will naturally conclude that eloquence is a much rarer commodity in England than in Italy.

LETTER LXI.

I have made two visits to Mount Vesuvius, the first in company with your acquaintance Mr. N——t. Leaving the carriage at Herculaneum, we mounted mules, and were attended by three men, whose business it is to accompany strangers up the mountain. Being arrived at a hermitage, called Il Salvatore, we found the road so broken and rough, that we thought proper to leave the mules at that place, which is inhabited by a French hermit. The poor man must have a very bad opinion of mankind, to choose the mouth of Mount Vesuvius for his nearest neighbour, in preference to their society. From the hermitage we walked over various fields of lava, which have burst out at different periods. These seemed to be perfectly well known to our guides, who mentioned their different dates as we passed. The latest appeared, before we left Rome, about two months ago; it was, however, but inconsiderable in comparison of other eruptions, there having been no bursting of the crater, or of the side of the mountain, as in the eruption of 1767, so well described by Sir William Hamilton; but only a boiling over of lava from the mouth of the volcano, and that not in excessive quantity; for it had done no damage to the vineyards or cultivated parts of the mountain, having reached no farther than the old black lava on which soil had not as yet been formed. I was surprised to see this lava of the last eruption still smoking, and in some places, where a considerable quantity was confined in a kind of deep path like a dry ditch, and shaded from the light of the Sun, it appeared of a glowing red colour. In other places, notwithstanding its being perfectly black and solid, it still retained such a degree of heat, that we could not stand upon it for any considerable time, but were obliged very frequently to step on the ground, or on older lava, to cool our feet. We had advanced a good way on a large piece of the latest lava, which was perfectly black and hard, and seemed cooler than the rest; while from this we looked at a stream of liquid lava, which flowed sluggishly along a hollow way at some distance. I accidentally threw my eyes below my feet, and perceived something, which mightily discomposed my contemplations. This was a small stream of the same matter, gliding to one side from beneath the black crust on which we stood. The idea of this crust giving way, and our sinking into the glowing liquid which it covered, made us shift our ground with great precipitation; which one of our guides observing, he called out, "Animo, animo, Signori;" and immediately jumped on the incrustation which we had abandoned, and danced above it, to shew that it was sufficiently strong, and that we had no reason to be afraid. We afterwards threw large stones of the heaviest kind we could find, into this rivulet, on whose surface they floated like cork in water; and on thrusting a stick into the stream, it required a considerable exertion of strength to make it enter. About this time the day began to overcast; this destroyed our hopes of enjoying the view from the top of the mountain, and we were not tempted to ascend any farther.

Some time after, I went to the summit with another party;—but I think it fair to inform you, that I have nothing new to say on the subject of volcanos, nor any philosophical remarks to make upon lavas. I have no guess of what time may be necessary for the formation of soil, nor do I know whether it accumulates in a regular progression, or is accelerated or retarded by various accidents, which may lead us into infinite errors, when we calculate time by such a rule. I have not the smallest wish to insinuate that the world is an hour older than Moses makes it; because I imagine those gentlemen whose calculations differ from his, are very nearly as liable to be mistaken as he was; because an attempt to prove it more ancient, can be no service to mankind; and finally, because, unless it could at the same time be proved that the world has acquired wisdom in proportion to its years, such an attempt conveys an oblique reflection on its character; for many follies may be overlooked and forgiven to a world of only five or six thousand years of age, which would be quite unpardonable at a more advanced period of existence. Having forewarned you that I shall treat of none of those matters, but simply describe what I saw, and mention perhaps a few incidents, none of which, I confess, are of great importance, I leave it in your choice to ascend the mountain with me, or not, as you please.

Having proceeded on mules as far as on the former occasion, we walked to that part of the mountain which is almost perpendicular. This appears of no great height, yet those who have never before attempted this ascent, fatigue themselves here much more than during all the rest of the journey, notwithstanding their being assisted by laying hold of the belts which the guides wear about their waists for that purpose. This part of the mountain appearing much shorter than it really is, people are tempted to make a violent effort, in the expectation of surmounting the difficulty at once; but the cinders, ashes, and other drossy materials, giving way, the foot generally sinks back two-thirds of each step; so that besides the height being greater than it appears, you have all the fatigue of ascending a hill three times as high as this is in reality. Those, therefore, who set out too briskly at first, and do not husband their strength at the beginning, have reason to repent their imprudence, being obliged to throw many a longing look, and make many a fruitless vow, before they, with the wretched guide who lugs them along, can arrive, panting and breathless, at the top; like those young men who, having wasted their vigour in early excesses, and brought on premature old age, link themselves to some ill-fated woman, who drags them, tormenting and tormented, to the grave.

Those who wish to view Mount Vesuvius to the greatest advantage, must begin their expedition in the evening; and the darker the succeeding night happens to be, so much the better. By the time our company had arrived at the top of the mountain, there was hardly any other light than that which issued by interrupted flashes from the volcano.

Exclusive of those periods when there are actual eruptions, the appearance and quantity of what issues from the mountain are very various; sometimes, for a long space of time together, it seems in a state of almost perfect tranquillity; nothing but a small quantity of smoke ascending from the volcano, as if that vast magazine of fuel, which has kept it alive for so many ages, was at last exhausted, and nothing remained but the dying embers; then, perhaps, when least expected, the cloud of smoke thickens, and is intermixed with flame; at other times, quantities of pumice stone and ashes are thrown up with a kind of hissing noise. For near a week the mountain has been more turbulent than at any time since the small eruption, or rather boiling over of lava, which took place about two months ago; and while we remained at the top, the explosions were of sufficient importance to satisfy our curiosity to the utmost. They appeared much more considerable there than we had imagined while at a greater distance; each of them was preceded by a noise like thunder within the mountain; a column of thick black smoke then issued out with great rapidity, followed by a blaze of flame; and immediately after, a shower of cinders and ashes, or red hot stones, were thrown into the sky. This was succeeded by a calm of a few minutes, during which nothing issued but a moderate quantity of smoke and flame, which gradually increased, and terminated in thunder and explosion as before. These accesses and intervals continued with varied force while we remained.

When we first arrived, our guides placed us at a reasonable distance from the mouth of the volcano, and on the side from which the wind came, so that we were no way incommoded by the smoke. In this situation the wind also bore to the opposite side the cinders, ashes, and other fiery substances, which were thrown up; and we ran no danger of being hurt, except when the explosion was very violent, and when red hot stones, and such heavy substances, were thrown like sky-rockets, with a great noise and prodigious force, into the air; and even these make such a flaming appearance, and take so much time in descending, that they are easily avoided.

Mr. Brydone, in his admirable account of Mount Ætna, tells us, he was informed, that, in an eruption of that mountain, large rocks of fire were discharged, with a noise much more terrible than that of thunder; that the person who informed him, reckoned from the time of their greatest elevation till they reached the ground, and found they took twenty-one seconds to descend; from whence he concludes their elevation had been seven thousand feet. This unquestionably required a power of projection far superior to what

Vesuvius has been known to exert. He himself measured the height of the explosions of the latter by the same rule; and the stones thrown the highest, never took above nine seconds to descend; which, by the same method of calculating, shews they had risen to little more than twelve hundred feet.— A pretty tolerable height, and might have satisfied the ambition of Vesuvius, if the stones of Ætna had not been said to have mounted so much higher. But before such an excessive superiority is granted to the latter, those who are acquainted with Mr. Brydone will recollect, that they have his own authority for the one fact, and that of another person for the other.

After having remained some time at the place where they were posted by the guides, our company grew bolder, as they became more familiarised to the object. Some made the circuit of the volcano, and by that means increased the risque of being wounded by the stones thrown out. Your young friend Jack was a good deal hurt by a fall, as he ran to avoid a large portion of some fiery substance, which seemed to be falling directly on his head.

Considering the rash and frolicsome disposition of some who visit this mountain, it is very remarkable that so few fatal accidents happen. I have heard of young English gentlemen betting, who should venture farthest, or remain longest, near the mouth of the Volcano. A very dreadful event had nearly taken place while our company remained. The bank, if it may be so called, on which some of them had stood when they looked into the Volcano, actually fell in before we left the summit of the mountain. This made an impression on all present, and inclined them to abandon so treacherous a neighbourhood. The steep hill of dross and cinders, which we had found it so difficult to ascend, we descended in a twinkling; but, as the night was uncommonly dark, we had much trouble in passing over the rough valley between that and the Hermitage, near which the mules waited. I ought to be ashamed, however, to mention the fatigue of this expedition; for two ladies, natives of Geneva, formed part of the company. One of them, big with child, accompanied her husband as far as the Hermitage, and was then with difficulty persuaded to go back; the other actually went to the summit, and returned with the rest of the company.

Before we set out for Naples, we were refreshed, at a little inn at the bottom of the mountain, with some glasses of a very generous and palatable wine, called *Lachrima Christi*; and experienced the truth of what an Italian Poet observed, that the effects of this wine form a strong contrast with its name:

Chi fu, de Contadini il più indiscreto,

Che à sbigottir la gente,

Diede nome dolente,

Al vin, che sopra ogn' altro il cuor fà lieto?

Lachrima dunque appellarassi un' riso,

Parto di nobilissima vindemia.

LETTER LXII.

Your account of our Friend's state of health gives me much concern; the more, as I cannot approve the change he has made of a physician. You say, the doctor, under whose care he is at present, has employed his mind so entirely in medical researches, that he scarcely displays a grain of common sense, when the conversation turns on any other subject; and that, although he seems opinionative, vain, and ostentatious in his profession, and full of false and absurd ideas in the common affairs of life, yet he is a very able physician, and has performed many wonderful cures. Be assured, my dear Sir, that this is impossible; for medical skill is not like the rod of an inchanter, which may be found accidentally, and which transfers its miraculous powers indiscriminately to a blockhead or a man of sense. The number of weak, gossipping men, who have made fortunes by this profession, do not prove the contrary. I do not say that men of that kind cannot make fortunes; I only assert they are not the most likely to cure diseases. An interest with apothecaries, nurses, and a few talkative old ladies, will enable them to do the first; but a clear understanding, and a considerable share of natural sagacity, are qualities essentially necessary for the second, and for every business which requires reflection. Without these, false inferences will be drawn from experience itself; and learning will tend to confirm a man in his errors, and to render him more completely a coxcomb.

The profession of physic is that, of all others, in which the generality of mankind have the fewest lights, by which they can discern the abilities of its professors; because the studies which lead to it are more out of the road of usual education, and the practice more enveloped in technical terms and hieroglyphical signs. But I imagine the safest criterion by which men, who have not been bred to that profession, can form a judgment of those who have, is, the degree of sagacity and penetration they discover on subjects equally open to mankind in general, and which ought to be understood by all who live in society. You do not mention particularly what has been prescribed by either; only that the former physician seemed to rely almost entirely on exercise and regimen, whereas the present flatters our friend with a speedy cure, by the help of the Pectoral and Balsamic medicines which he orders in such abundance, and which he declares are so efficacious in *pulmonary consumptions*.

Having lamented with you the mournful events which render the name of that disease peculiarly alarming to you, and knowing your friendly solicitude about Mr. ——, I do not wonder at your earnest desire to know something of the nature of a distemper with which he is threatened, and which has proved fatal to so many of our friends. But I am surprised that you have not chosen a more enlightened instructor, when you have so many around you. Though conscious that I have no just claim to all the obliging expressions which your partiality to my opinions has prompted you to make use of, yet I am too much flattered by some of them, to refuse complying with your request. My sentiments, such as they are, will at least have the merit of being clearly understood. I shall observe your prohibition, not to refer you to any medical book; and shall carefully avoid all technical terms, which you so much abominate. With regard to your shewing my Letter to any of the faculty; if you find yourself so inclined, I have not the smallest objection; for those who have the greatest knowledge in their profession, are best acquainted with its uncertainty, and most indulgent to the mistakes or errors of others.

Alas, my friend! how is it possible that physicians should avoid mistakes? If the ablest mechanic were to attempt to remedy the irregular movements of a watch, while he remained ignorant of the structure and manner of acting of some of the principal springs, would he not be in danger of doing harm instead of good? Physicians are in the situation of such a mechanic; for, although it is evident that the nerves are the organs of motion and sensation, yet their structure is not known. Some anatomists assert they are impervious cords; others, that they are slender tubes, containing a fluid. But what the nature of this fluid is; whether it serves only to nourish the nerves themselves, or is the medium by which they convey feeling and the power of motion to other parts, is not ascertained even by those who argue for its existence; far less is it explained in what manner ideas, formed within the brain, can, by the means of solid cords, or by a fluid contained in tubes, communicate motion at pleasure to the legs and arms. We are ignorant why the will, which has no influence over the motion of an animal's heart, should find the feet obedient to her dictates; and we can no more explain how a man can move one leg over the other by volition, or the mere act of willing, than how he could, by the same means, move Ossa on the top of Olympus. The one happens every moment, the other would be considered as a miracle; but they are equally unaccountable. While parts so infinitely essential to life are not understood, instead of being surprised that so many diseases baffle the skill of the physician, we have more reason to be astonished that any can be alleviated or cured by his art.

The pen of the satirist, no doubt, may be fairly aimed against the presumption and ignorance of many individuals of this, as of every other profession; but cannot with justice be directed against the art itself: since, in spite of the obscurity which still involves some parts of the animal economy, many disorders are relieved, and some of the severest and most disagreeable to which the human body is liable, are cured with certainty by the art of medicine.

Unfortunately for mankind, and in a particular manner for the inhabitants of Great Britain, the pulmonary consumption is not of the number.

This disease may originate from various causes:

1st. An external bruise or wound.

2d. The disease called pleurisy, including in that term an inflammation of the lungs themselves, as well as the membrane which covers them.

3d. The bursting of some of the blood-vessels of the lungs, independent of external injury, and owing to a faulty conformation of the chest, and the slenderness of the vessels.

4th. Certain small tumours, called tubercles, in the lungs.

The first cause I have mentioned is an external bruise or wound.

An accident of that kind happening to the lungs, is more dangerous and difficult to cure, than when the same takes place in most other parts of the body; because the lungs are vital organs, essentially necessary to life, and when their motion is impaired, other animal functions are thereby injured; because they are of an uncommonly delicate texture, in which a rupture having once taken place, will be apt to increase; because they are in constant motion and exposed to the access of external air, both of which circumstances are unfavourable to the healing of wounds, and because the mass of blood distributed to the whole body passes previously through the lungs, and consequently the blood-vessels of this organ are more numerous than those of any other part of the body.

When we consider these peculiarities, it is natural to conclude, that every wound of the lungs must necessarily prove mortal; but experience has taught the contrary. Many wounds of the lungs heal of themselves, by what is called, the first intention. The physician may prevent a fever, by ordering the patient to lose blood in proper quantities, and he may regulate the diet; but the cure must be left to nature, which she will perform with greater certainty, if she is not disturbed by any of those balsams which the wounded are sometimes directed to swallow on such occasions. But when the wound, either from injudicious treatment, or from its size, or from the bad habit of the patient, degenerates into an ulcer attended with hectic symptoms, the disease must be treated as if it had arisen from any of the other causes.

The pleurisy, or inflammation of the lungs, is a disease more frequent in cold countries than in mild; in the spring than in the other seasons; and more apt to seize people of a sanguine constitution than others.

Plentiful and repeated bleedings, fomentations, blisters near the affected part, and a cooling, diluting regimen, generally remove it, without its leaving any bad consequence. Sometimes, by the omission of bleeding in due quantity at the beginning, and sometimes in spite of all possible care, it terminates in an abscess, which, on bursting, may suffocate the patient; or, if the matter is coughed up, becomes an open ulcer, and produces the disease in question.

The third cause of the pulmonary consumption above mentioned, is, a spitting of blood, from the bursting of vessels of the lungs, independent of external wound or bruise. People of a fair complexion, delicate skin, slender make, long neck, and narrow chest, are more subject to this than others. Those who have a predisposition to this complaint, by their form, are most apt to be attacked after their full growth: women from fifteen to three-and-thirty; men two or three years later. In Great Britain, a spitting of blood generally occurs to those predisposed to it, in the spring, or beginning of summer, when the weather suddenly changes from cold to excessive hot; and when the heat is supposed to rarify the blood, before the solids are proportionably relaxed from the contracted state they acquire during the cold of winter. When a spitting of blood happens to a person who has actually lost brothers or sisters, or other near relations, by the pulmonary consumption, as that circumstance gives reason to suspect a family taint or predisposition, the case will, on that account, be more dangerous.

Violent exercise may occasion the rupture of blood-vessels in the lungs, even in those who have no hereditary disposition to such an accident; it ought therefore to be carefully avoided by all who have. Violent exercise, in the spring, is more dangerous than in other seasons; and, when taken at the top of high mountains, by those who do not usually reside there, it has been considered as more dangerous than in vallies. The sudden diminution of the weight of the atmosphere, co-operating with the exercise, renders the vessels more apt to break. Of all things the most pernicious to people predisposed to a spitting of blood, is, playing upon wind-instruments. Previous to the spitting of blood, some perceive an uneasiness in the chest, an oppression on the breath, and a saltish taste in the spittle; but these symptoms are not constant.

Nothing can be more insidious than the approaches of this disease sometimes are. The substance of the lungs, which is so full of blood-vessels, is not supplied so liberally with nerves; the lungs, therefore, may be materially affected, before danger is indicated by acute pain. And it sometimes happens, that people of the make above described are, in the bloom of life, and generally in the spring of the year, seized with a slight cough, which gradually increases, without pain, soreness in the breast, difficulty of respiration, or spitting of blood. A slow fever supervenes every night, which remits every morning, with sweats. These symptoms augment daily; and, in spite of early attention, and what is thought the best advice, the unsuspecting victims gradually sink into their graves.

Those who by their make, or by the disease having in former instances appeared in their family, are predisposed to this complaint, ought to be peculiarly attentive in the article of diet. A spare and cooling regimen is the best. They should avoid violent exercise, and every other exciting cause; and use the precaution of losing blood in the spring. If their circumstances permit, they ought to pass the cold months in a mild climate; but, if they are obliged to remain during the winter in Great Britain, let them wear flannel next the skin, and use every other precaution against catching colds.

The fourth cause above enumerated is, tubercles in the lungs.

The moist, soggy, and changeable weather, which prevails in Great Britain, renders its inhabitants more liable, than those of milder and more uniform climates, to catarrhs, rheumatisms, pleurisies, and other diseases proceeding from obstructed perspiration. The same cause subjects the inhabitants of Great Britain to obstructions of the glands, scrophulous complaints, and tubercles in the substance of the lungs. The scrophulous disease is more frequent than is generally imagined. For one person in whom it appears by swellings in the glands below the chin, and other external marks, many have the internal glands affected by it. This is well known to those who are accustomed to open dead bodies. On examining the bodies of such as have died of the pulmonary consumption, besides the open ulcers in the lungs, many little hard tumours or tubercles are generally found; some, with matter; others, on being cut open, discover a little blueish spot, of the size of a small lead shot. Here the suppuration, or formation of matter, is just going to begin; and in some the tubercle is perfectly hard, and the colour whitish, throughout its whole substance. Tubercles may remain for a considerable time in the lungs, in this indolent state, without much inconveniency; but, when excited to inflammation by frequent catarrhs, or other irritating causes, matter is formed, they break, and produce an ulcer. Care and attention may prevent tubercles from inflammation, or may prevent *that* from terminating in the formation of matter; but when matter is actually formed, and the tubercle has become an abscess, no remedy can stop its progress. It must go on till it bursts. If this happens near any of the large air-vessels, immediate suffocation may ensue; but, for the most part, the matter is coughed up.

From the circumstances above enumerated of the delicate texture, constant motion, and numerous blood-vessels of the lungs, it is natural to imagine, that a breach of this nature in their substance will be still more difficult to heal than a wound from an external cause. So unquestionably it is; yet there are many instances of even this kind of breach being repaired; the matter expectorated diminishing in quantity every day, and the ulcer gradually healing; not, surely, by the power of medicine, but by the constant disposition and tendency which exists in nature, by inscrutable means of her own, to restore health to the human body.

It may be proper to observe, that those persons whose formation of body renders them most liable to a spitting of blood, have also a greater predisposition than others to tubercles in the lungs. The disease, called the spasmodic asthma, has been reckoned among the causes of the pulmonary consumption. It would require a much greater degree of confidence in a man's own judgment, than I have in mine, to assert, that this complaint has no tendency to produce tubercles in the lungs; but I may say, with truth, that I have often known the spasmodic asthma, in the most violent degree, attended with the most alarming symptoms, continue to harass the patients for a long period of time, and at length suddenly disappear, without ever returning; the persons who have been thus afflicted, enjoying perfect health for many years after. It is not probable that tubercles were formed in any of these cases; and it is certain they were not in some, whose bodies were opened after their deaths, which happened from other distempers, the asthma having disappeared several years before.

Certain eruptions of the skin, attended with fever, particularly the small-pox, and still oftener the measles, leave after them a foundation for the pulmonary consumption. From whichever of the causes above enumerated this disease takes its origin, when once an ulcer, attended with a hectic fever, is formed in the lungs, the case is, in the highest degree, dangerous. When it ends fatally, the symptoms are, a quick pulse, and a sensation of cold, while the patient's skin, to the feeling of every other person, is hot; irregular shiverings, a severe cough, expectoration of matter streaked with blood, morning sweats, a circumscribed spot of a crimson colour on the cheeks, heat of the palms of the hands, excessive emaciation, crooking of the nails, swelling of the legs, giddiness, delirium, soon followed by death.

These symptoms do not appear in every case. Although the emaciation is greater in this disease than in any other, yet the appetite frequently remains strong and unimpaired to the last; and although delirium sometimes comes before death, yet in many cases the senses seem perfect and intire; except in one particular, that in spite of all the foregoing symptoms, the patient often entertains the fullest hopes of recovery to the last moment.

Would to heaven it were as easy to point out the cure, as to describe the symptoms of a disease of such a formidable nature, and against which the powers of medicine have been directed with such bad success, that there is reason to fear, its fatal termination has been oftener accelerated than retarded by the means employed to remove it! To particularise the drugs which have been long in use, and have been honoured with the highest encomiums for their great efficacy in healing inward bruises, ulcers of the lungs, and confirmed consumptions, would in many instances be pointing out, what ought to be shunned as pernicious, and in others what ought to be neglected as futile.

Salt water, and some of the mineral springs, which are unquestionably beneficial in scrophulous and other distempers, have been found hurtful, or at least inefficacious, in the consumption; there is no sufficient reason to depend on a course of these, or any medicine at present known, for preventing or dissolving tubercles in the lungs. Mercury, which has been found so powerful in disposing other ulcers to heal, has no good effect on ulcers of that organ;—though some physicians imagine it may be of service in the beginning to dissolve tubercles, before they begin to suppurate; but as there is no absolute evidence, during life, of indolent tubercles being formed, there can be none that mercury cures them.

Various kinds of gums, with the natural and artificial balsams, were long supposed to promote the healing of external wounds and ulcers, and on that account were made the basis of a vast variety of ointments and plaisters. It was afterwards imagined, that the same remedies, administered internally, would have the same effect on internal ulcers; and of course many of those gums and balsams were prescribed in various forms for the pulmonary consumption. The reasoning on which this practice was established, however, seems a little shallow, and is far from being conclusive; for although it were granted, that these balsams contributed to the cure of wounds, when applied directly to the part, it does not follow that they could carry their healing powers, unimpaired, from the stomach to the lungs, through the whole process of digestion. But more accurate surgery having made it manifest, that the granulations which spring up to supply the loss of substance in external wounds, and the healing or skinning over of all kinds of sores, proceeds from no active virtue in the plaisters or ointments with which they are dressed, but is entirely the work of nature, and best performed when the mildest substances, or even dry lint only is applied; and that heating gums, resins, and balsams, rather retard than promote their cure; the internal use of such remedies ought to be rejected now, on the same principles they were adapted formerly.

No kind of reasoning ought to have weight, when opposed by fair experience. But physicians have formed contrary and opposite conclusions, with respect to the effect of the natural and artificial balsams, even when they have laid all theory and reasoning aside, and decided on their powers from practice and experiment only. This is sufficient to prove, at least, that their efficacy is very problematical. For my own part, after the fairest trials, and the most accurate observations I have been able to make, I cannot say that I ever knew them of service in any hectic complaint proceeding from an ulcer in the lungs; and I have generally found those physicians, on whose judgment I have more reliance than on my own, of the same opinion.

It is far from being uncommon to see a cure retarded, not to say any thing stronger, by the means employed to hasten it; and physicians who found their practice on theoretical reasonings, are not the only persons to whom this misfortune may happen. Those who profess to take experience for their sole guide, if it is not directed by candour, and enlightened by natural sagacity, are liable to the same. A man may, for twenty years, order a medicine, which has in every instance done a little harm, though not always so much as to prevent nature from removing the complaint at last; and if the reputation of this medicine should ever be attacked, he may bring his twenty years experience in support of it. It ought to be remembered, that as often as the animal constitution is put out of order, by accident or distemper, nature endeavours to restore health. Happily she has many resources, and various methods of accomplishing her purpose; and very often she succeeds best without medical assistance. But medical assistance being given, she frequently succeeds *notwithstanding*; and it sometimes happens, that both physician and patient are convinced, that the means which did not prevent have actually performed the cure.

A peasant is seized with a shivering, followed by feverishness, and accompanied with a slight cough—he goes to bed, and excessive heat and thirst prompt him to drink plentifully of plain water; on the second or third day a copious sweat bursts from all his pores, and terminates the disorder. A person of fortune is seized with the same symptoms, arising from the same cause, and which would have been cured by the same means, in the same space of time; but the apothecary is called, who immediately sends pectoral linctuses to remove the cough, and afterwards gives a vomit, to remove the nausea which the linctuses have occasioned: the heat and fever augment; the physician is called; he orders the patient to be blooded, to abate the violence of the fever, and gives a little physic on some other account. All this prevents the natural crisis by sweat; and the patient being farther teased by draughts or powders every two or three hours, nature cannot shake off the fever so soon by six or seven days, as she would have done had she been left to herself. She generally does her business at last, however; and then the physician and apothecary glory in the happy effects of their skill, and receive the grateful thanks of their patient for having cured him of a dangerous fever.

Every body of common penetration, at all conversant in medical matters, must have seen enough to convince them that the above description is not exaggerated; but it is not to be inferred from this, that the art of medicine is of no use to mankind. There are many diseases in which nature sinks, without medical assistance. It is the part of the penetrating and experienced physician to distinguish these from others, and leave it to the knavish and weak to assume the merit of cures in cases where they know, or ought to know, that medicine can do nothing.

Some physicians, who have abandoned the other resins and gums, as useless or hurtful in hectic complaints, still adhere to myrrh as a beneficial medicine; but from what I can learn, the cases in which this gum has been thought serviceable, are hectic complaints, from debility, in consequence of excessive evacuations of various kinds, and not proceeding from ulcerated lungs. After it is fully established that myrrh is of use in such instances, it will still be worthy of investigation, whether it is of more or less than Jesuits bark. I have repeatedly mentioned blood-letting, and a spare, diluting regimen, as the most powerful means of preventing and curing all affections of the lungs that depend on inflammation. In the case of external wounds, or bruises of the lungs, this method facilitates the immediate cure by the first intention. It is the chief thing to be depended on for the cure of pleurisies; and it is often owing to a neglect, or too sparing an use of this evacuation, that the complaint terminates in an abscess. In people predisposed by the form of their bodies, or the nature of their constitutions, to a spitting of blood, it may prevent the turgid vessels from bursting; and in those who have tubercles in the lungs, it is of the greatest utility, by preventing those tumours from inflaming, and becoming ulcers; but after the ulcers are actually formed, I have great doubts with regard to the propriety of attempting a cure by repeated bleedings, even in small quantities. This method has been often tried; but I fear the success with which it has been attended, gives no encouragement to continue the practice. That symptoms may be such, in every period of this disease, as to require this evacuation, is not to be denied; but there is a great difference in the application of what is considered as an occasional palliative, and that from which we expect a radical cure. In the one case, it will only be used when some particular symptom strongly urges; in the other, it will be used at stated intervals, whether the symptoms press or not; and may tend to weaken the already debilitated patient, without our having the consolation of knowing, with certainty, that it has had any other effect.

Blisters do not weaken so much; they are of undoubted use in pleurisies; perhaps, by exciting external inflammation, they may contribute to draw off the inflammatory disposition within the breast: perhaps—But in whatever way they act, I imagine I have frequently seen blisters and setons, particularly the latter, of considerable service, even after the symptoms indicated the existence of an ulcer in the lungs.

As for the numerous forms of electuaries, lohochs, and linctuses, composed of oils, gums, and syrups, and by the courtesy of dispensatory writers called *pectoral*; I am convinced they are of no manner of service in this complaint, and seldom have any other effect than that of loading the stomach, and impairing the digestion of salutary food. So far from being of any permanent service to the disease, they cannot be depended on for giving even a temporary relief to the cough; when that symptom becomes troublesome, gentle opiates will be found the best palliatives. Some practitioners object to these medicines, on a supposition that they check expectoration; but they only seem to have this effect, by lulling the irritation to cough; the same quantity will be expectorated in the morning, after the influence of the opiate is over. It is surely better that the matter should accumulate, and the patient spit it up at once, than allow him to be kept from rest, and teased with coughing and spitting through the whole night. These palliatives, however, are to be managed with great caution; never exhibited while the patient enjoys a tolerable share of *natural* rest. Small doses should be given at first, and not increased without absolute necessity. Exhibited in this manner, they cannot do harm; and those who reject the assistance of a class of medicines, which afford ease and tranquillity in the most deplorable state of this disease, ought to give better proofs than have hitherto appeared, that they are able to procure their patients more valuable and lasting comforts than those they deprive them of.

The known efficacy of the Peruvian bark, in many distempers, especially in intermittent fevers; the remission of the symptoms, which happens regularly every day at a particular stage of the pulmonary consumption, and in some degree gives it the appearance of an intermittent, joined to the failure of all other remedies, prompted physicians to make trial of that noble medicine in this disease. In consequence of these trials, the bark is now pretty generally acknowledged to be serviceable in hectical complaints, proceeding from debility, and other causes, exclusive of ulcerated lungs; but when the disease proceeds from this cause, the bark is supposed, by some very respectable physicians, always to do harm. I am most clearly of the first opinion, and perhaps it would not become me to dispute the second. It may be permitted, however, to observe, that the most discerning practitioners may be led into a notion, that a very safe medicine does harm, when it is exhibited at the worst stage of a disease, in which hardly any medicine whatever has been found to do good. In every stage of this disease, elixir of vitriol may be used. It is a pleasant and safe medicine, but particularly efficacious when the patient is troubled with wasting sweats.

Having, in obedience to your request, delivered my sentiments freely, you will perceive, that, besides the objections already mentioned to the person under whose care our friend is at present, I cannot approve of his being directed to take so many drugs, or of his being detained in town, at a season when he may enjoy, in the country, what is preferable to all medicine; I mean air, exercise, and, let me even add, diet.

Had I known of our friend's complaints earlier, I should have advised him to have met the advancing spring in the South of France; but at the season in which you will receive this letter, the moderate warmth, and refreshing verdure of England, are preferable to the sultry heats and scorched fields of the South. From the view I have of his complaints, I can have no hesitation in advising you to endeavour to prevail on him to quit his drugs, and to leave London without delay. Since he bears riding on horseback so well, let him enjoy that exercise in an atmosphere freed from the smoke of the town, and impregnated with the flavour of rising plants and green herbage; a flavour which may with more truth be called *pectoral*, than any of the heating resins, or loathsome oils, on which that term has been prostituted. Let him pass the summer in drinking the waters, and riding around the environs of Bristol. It will be easy for him to find a house in the free air of the country, at some distance from that town; and it will be of use to have an additional reason for rising early, and riding every morning. It is of the greatest importance that he continue that exercise every day that the weather will permit: a little cloudiness of the sky should not fright him from it; there is no danger of catching cold during the continuation of that movement which assists digestion, promotes the determination of blood from the lungs to the surface of the body, and is more salutary in the morning than after dinner.

With respect to diet, he should carefully observe the important rule of taking food frequently, in small quantities, and never making a full meal; that the digestive organs may not be overpowered, or the vessels charged with too large a quantity of chyle at a time; which never fails to bring on oppressive breathing, and augments the fever and flushing, which in some degree succeeds every repast.

Since all kinds of milk are found to disagree with his constitution, that nourishment, which is in general so well adapted to similar complaints, must be omitted, and light broths, with vegetable food, particularly of the farinaceous kind, substituted in its place.

Acids, especially the native acid of vegetables, are remarkably agreeable and refreshing to all who labour under the heat, oppression, and languor, which accompany hectic complaints. It is surprising what a quantity of the juice of lemons the constitution will bear, without any inconveniency, when it is accustomed to it by degrees; and in those cases where it does not occasion pains in the stomach and bowels, or other immediate inconveniencies, it has been thought to have a good effect in abating the force of the hectic fever.

I have met with two cases, since I have been last abroad, in both of which there seemed to be a quicker recovery than I ever saw, from the same symptoms. The first was that of a young lady, of about seventeen years of age, and apparently of a very healthy constitution. In bad weather, during the spring, she caught cold: this being neglected in the beginning, gradually grew worse. When physicians were at length consulted, their prescriptions seemed to have as bad an effect as her own neglect. By the middle of summer her cough was incessant, accompanied with hectic fever and flushings, irregular shiverings, morning sweats, emaciation, expectoration of purulent phlegm streaked with blood, and every indication of an open ulcer in the lungs. In this desperate state she was carried from the town to a finely situated village in Switzerland, where, for several months, she lived in the middle of a vineyard, on ripe grapes and bread. She had been directed to a milk and vegetable diet in general. Her own taste inclined her to the grapes, which she continued, on finding, that, with this diet only, she was less languid, and of a more natural coolness, and that the cough, fever, and all the other symptoms gradually abated. She seemed to be brought from the jaws of death by the change of air, and this regimen only; and she returned to her own home in high spirits, and with the look and vigour of health. The ensuing winter, after being heated with dancing at the house of a friend, she walked home in a cold night; the cough, spitting of blood, and other symptoms immediately returned, and she died three months after.

In the other case, there was not such a degree of fever, but there was an expectoration of matter, frequently streaked with blood, and evident signs of an ulcer in the lungs. The person who laboured under these symptoms, had tried the usual remedies of pectorals, pills, linctuses, &c. with the usual success. He grew daily worse. He had formerly found much relief from bleeding, but had left it off for many months, on a supposition that it had lost all effect; and he had allowed an issue to be healed, on the same supposition; though he still persevered in a milk regimen. I mentioned to him the case of the young lady, as it is above recited. He immediately took the resolution to confine himself to bread and grapes for almost his only food. I advised him at the same time to have the issue opened, and to continue that drain for some time; but this he did not comply with. He forsook, however, the town for the country, and passed as much of the morning on horseback, as he could bear without fatigue. He soon was able to bear more; and after about three weeks or a month, his cough had greatly abated. When he had persisted in this regimen between two and three months, he had very little cough; and what he spit up was pure phlegm, unmixed with blood or matter. He has now been well above a year; and although I understand that he occasionally takes animal food, he has hitherto felt no inconveniency from it. He passed the second autumn, as he had done the first, at a house in the country, surrounded with vineyards. The greater part of his food consisted of ripe grapes and bread. With such a diet, he had not occasion for much drink of any kind; what he used was simple water, and he made an ample provision of grapes for the succeeding winter.

Though I have no idea that there is any specific virtue in grapes, for the cure of the pulmonary consumption, or that they are greatly preferable to some other cooling, sub-acid, mild fruit, equally agreeable to the taste, provided any such can be found; yet I thought it right to particularize what was used on those two occasions; leaving it to others to determine, what share of the happy consequences I have enumerated were owing to the change of air, how much may have flowed from the exercise, how much from the regimen, and whether there is reason to think, that the favourable turn in both cases depended on other circumstances, unobserved by me.

I have now, my dear Sir, complied with your request; and although I have endeavoured to avoid technical verbosity, and all unnecessary detail, yet I find my letter has swelled to a greater size than I expected. I shall be exceedingly happy to hear that any hint I have given has been serviceable to our friend. If the cough should still continue, after he has passed two or three months at Bristol, I imagine the most effectual thing he can do will be, to take a voyage to this place; he will by that means escape the severity of a British winter. The voyage itself will be of service, and at the end of it he will have the benefit of the mild air of the Campagna Felice, be refreshed and nourished by the finest grapes, and, when tired of riding, he will have continual opportunities of sailing in this charming bay.

LETTER LXIII.

As I was walking a few days since in the street with two of our countrymen, T—— and N——, we met some people carrying the corpse of a man on an open bier, and others following in a kind of procession. The deceased was a tradesman, whose widow had bestowed the utmost attention in dressing him to the greatest advantage on this solemn occasion; he had a perfectly new suit of clothes, a laced hat upon his head, ruffles, his hair finely powdered, and a large blooming nosegay in his left hand, while the right was very gracefully stuck in his side. It is the custom at Naples to carry every body to church in full dress soon after their death, and the nearest relations display the magnitude of their grief by the magnificent manner in which they decorate the corpse. This poor woman, it seems, was quite inconsolable, and had ornamented the body of her late husband with a profusion she could ill afford. When the corpse arrives in church, the service is read over it. That ceremony being performed, and the body carried home, it is considered as having no farther occasion for fine clothes, but is generally stript to the shirt, and buried privately.

"Can any thing be more ridiculous," says N——, "than to trick a man out in his bed clothes after his death?" "Nothing," replied T——; "unless it be to order a fantastical dress at a greater expence on purpose, as if the dead would not be satisfied with the clothes they wore when alive, but delighted in long flowing robes in a particular style of their own."

T—— has long resided abroad, and now prefers many foreign customs to those of his own country, which frequently involves him in disputes with his countrymen.

The Princess of —— drove past. "There she goes," says N——, "with her cavalieros, her volantis, and all the splendour of a sovereign; yet the wife of a plain English gentleman is in a far more enviable situation. With all her titles and her high rank, she is a meer servant of the Queen's, a dependant on the caprice of another; a frown from her Majesty would annihilate her." "Those who are *nothing*, exclusive of court favour," replied T——, "ought not be censured for devoting their time to court attendance. But did you never hear of any who are dazzled with the glitter of court shackels in the boasted land of liberty; people whom riches, rank, and the most flattering favours of fortune cannot make independent; whose minds seem the more abject, as their situation lays them under the less necessity of remaining in servitude; who, withered with age, and repining with envy, sacrifice every domestic duty, and stalk around the mansions of royalty, as ghosts are said to haunt those abodes in which they most delighted when they enjoyed life and vigour?" "Well, well," says N——, "let us say no more about them, since we are agreed, that, of all the old tapestry of courts, those grotesque figures, who, without the confidence of those they serve, continue to the last exhibiting their antique countenances at birthday balls, and in the assemblies of youth and beauty, are the most ridiculous." At that instant the Queen passed in her coach with the royal children, and N—— made some comparative remarks in his usual style; to which T—— replied, "In this particular I acknowledge the happiness of Great Britain. I presume not to make comparisons; the great character you have mentioned defies censure, and is far superior to my praise. But I must observe, it appears singular that you, who affect to despise all other countries, and seem of opinion, that what is most valuable in nature is always the product of *England*, should bring your brightest illustration of that opinion from *Germany*."

T——, perceiving the advantage he had gained over his antagonist, proceeded vigorously to censure, what he called, the absurd partiality of the English in their own favour; and observed, that it would be fortunate for them, if the other nations of Europe would allow them but a few of the numerous good qualities which they so lavishly attribute to themselves. He severely attacked the common people, and denied them even the character of good-nature, which they have been thought to possess in an eminent degree. He declared them to be rough and insolent in their manners (for the truth of this he appealed to the opinion of all their neighbours), cruel in their dispositions (as a proof of which he instanced some of their favourite diversions), and absurd in their prejudices, which appears by their hatred and contempt of other nations; by all of whom, he asserted, they were in return most cordially abhorred. "How, indeed, can it be otherwise," continued he, "considering the rough, boisterous nature of their weather?" He then expatiated on the fertility of Italy, and the mild serenity of the climate; to which he partly attributed the fertile genius and mild character of the Italians. "No doubt," he said, "moral causes might contribute to the same effect; for more pains were taken to cultivate and encourage good and quiet dispositions in the common people here than in England. They were accustomed to perform their religious duties more regularly; they had frequent opportunities of hearing the most excellent music in the churches; they were instructed in history by orators in the street, and were made acquainted with the beauties of their best poets in the same manner. All these causes united must necessarily enlarge their minds, and make them the most gentle, humane, and ingenious people in the world." N—— shook his head, as if he laid little stress on the others reasoning. For my own part, I remained silent, being desirous that the dispute should go on between the two who had begun it.

Continuing our walk a little without the town, we saw a crowd of people looking over a wall, which formed one side of a square, expressly built for the purpose of bating cattle with bull dogs. It is imagined that this renders their flesh more tender and agreeable to the taste; and this is considered as a sufficient reason for torturing great numbers of bulls, oxen, and cows, before they are slaughtered for the markets; we found a multitude of spectators enjoying this amusement. "Pray," says Mr. N——, addressing himself to T——, "do you imagine this humane practice, and the complacency which these refined spectators seem to take in beholding it, proceed from the mildness of the climate, the pains bestowed in teaching the people the duties of christianity, the enlargement of their minds by history and poetry, or from the gentle influence of music upon their dispositions?" Then turning from Mr. T—— to me, he continued, "Not satisfied with knocking the poor animals on the head, those unfeeling epicures put them to an hour's additional torture, merely to gratify a caprice of their corrupted palates."

"Of all subjects," replied T——, recovering himself from the confusion into which N——'s questions had thrown him, "those who take upon them to be the panegyrists of the English nation, ought to avoid mentioning that species of epicurism which depends on eating, lest they be put in mind of whipping pigs to death, their manner of collaring brawn, crimping fish, and other refinements peculiar to that humane good-natured people."

N—— was just going to reply, when a large bull, rendered outrageous by the stones which the populace were throwing at him, ran suddenly towards the gate at the instant the keepers were opening it on some other account; which threw them into such confusion, that they had not time to shut it before the bull burst out on the multitude. He now became an object of terror to those who the moment before had looked on him as an object of mirth. The mighty lords of the creation, who consider other animals as formed entirely for *their pastime, their attire, their food,* fled in crowds from one quadruped, and would gladly have fallen on their knees and worshipped him, like so many Egyptians adoring Apis, if by so doing they could have hoped to deprecate the just wrath of the incensed animal.—They found safety at length, not in their own courage or address, but in the superior boldness and agility of other animals, who were leagued with man against him. He was surrounded by dogs, who attacked him on all sides—he killed some outright, tossed and wounded many more; but perceiving his own strength diminishing, and the number of his enemies increasing every moment, he threw himself into the sea, and there found a temporary protection from the fury of his persecutors.—But the dogs were instigated to follow; they at length drove him from this last asylum; and the poor, torn, bleeding, exhausted animal was forced ashore, three or four of the most furious of the dogs hanging at different parts of his head and neck. When they were removed, he raised his honest countenance, and threw an indignant look upon the rabble, as if to upbraid them for such a return for his own labours, and all the essential services which his whole species render to mankind. Upon my soul I felt the reproach. We could not bear his looks, but sneaked away without feeling much pride on account of our near connection with those lords of the creation, whom we had just beheld exerting their prerogative.

We walked along a considerable time without speaking. N—— broke silence at last: "Well," said he, "those amiable creatures whom we have quitted, are what they call human beings;—they are more, they are Neapolitans, men who are moved with the concord of sweet sounds; from which I conclude (Shakespear may say what he pleases), that such men are as fit for treasons, stratagems, and spoils, as those who never heard softer melody than that of marrow-bones and cleavers."

"This fondness for barbarous amusements," said I, "cannot be stated exclusively to the account of Neapolitans, of English, or of any other particular people. I am afraid the charge lies against mankind in general; from whatever motive it arises, a large proportion of the individuals in all countries have displayed a decided taste for diversions which may be ranged in this class."

"It ought to be remembered, however," says T——, "that those fellows with their dogs, who have been tormenting the bull, are butchers, and the lowest of the vulgar of this country; whereas, among those who order fish to be crimped, and pigs to be whipped to death, as well as among those who formerly attended Broughton's amphitheatre, and still attend cockpits, will be found people of the first rank in England."

"Pray," said N——, addressing himself to me, "did you ever see a cocagna?"

I acknowledged I never had.

"Then," continued he, "I beg leave to give you an idea of it. It is a Neapolitan entertainment, relished by people of the first rank in this polished country; where the very vagrants in the street are instructed in history, and the human mind is refined by poetry, softened by music, and elevated by religion. The cocagna—Pray mark me—the cocagna is an entertainment given to the people four succeeding Sundays during the carnival. Opposite to the palace, a kind of wooden amphitheatre is erected. This being covered with branches of trees, bushes, and various plants, real and artificial, has the appearance of a green hill. On this hill are little buildings, ornamented with pillars of loaves of bread, with joints of meat, and dried fish, varnished, and curiously arranged by way of capitals. Among the trees and bushes are some oxen, a considerable number of calves, sheep, hogs, and lambs, all alive, and tied to posts. There are, besides, a great number of living turkies, geese, hens, pigeons, and other fowls, nailed by the wings to the scaffolding. Certain Heathen Deities appear also occasionally upon this hill, but not with a design to protect it, as you shall see immediately. The guards are drawn up in three ranks, to keep off the populace. The Royal Family, with all the nobility of the court, crowd the windows and balconies of the palace, to enjoy this magnificent sight. When his Majesty waves his handkerchief, the guards open to the right and left; the rabble pour in from all quarters, and the entertainment commences. You may easily conceive what a delightful sight it must be, to see several thousand hungry, half-naked lazzaroni rush in like a torrent, destroy the whole fabric of loaves, fishes, and joints of meat; overturn the Heathen Deities, *for the honour of Christianity*; pluck the fowls, at the expence of their wings, from the posts to which they were nailed; and, in the fury of their struggling and fighting for their prey, often tearing the miserable animals to pieces, and sometimes stabbing each other."

"You ought, in candour, to add," interrupted Mr. T——, "that, though formerly they were fixed to the posts alive, yet of late the larger cattle have been previously killed."—"And pray, my good Sir," said N——, "will you be so obliging as to inform me, what crime the poor lambs and fowls have committed, that they should be torn in pieces alive?" "This piece of humanity," continued he, "recalls to my memory a similar instance, in a certain ingenious gentleman, who proposed, as the best and most effectual method of sweeping chimnies, to place a large goose at the top; and then, by a string tied around her feet, to pull the animal gently down to the hearth. The sagacious projector asserted, that the goose, being extremely averse to this method of entering a house, would struggle against it with all her might; and, during this resistance, would move her wings with such force and rapidity, as could not fail to sweep the chimney completely." "Good God, Sir," cried a lady, who was present when this new method was proposed, "How cruel would that be to the poor goose!" "Why, Madam," replied the gentleman, "if you think my method cruel to the goose, a couple of ducks will do."

LETTER LXIV.

On the first Sunday of May, we had an opportunity of seeing the famous Neapolitan miracle, of the liquefaction of Saint Januarius's blood, performed. This Saint, you know, is the patron of Naples; which circumstance alone forms a strong presumption of his being a Saint of very considerable power and efficacy; for it is not to be imagined that the care of a city, like Naples, which is threatened every moment with destruction from Mount Vesuvius, would be entrusted to an under-strapper. Indeed there has, on some occasions, been reason to fear, that, great and powerful as this Saint is, the Dæmon of the mountain would have got the better of him; however, as Saint Januarius has been able to protect them hitherto, and is supposed to be improved in the science of defence by long practice, the Neapolitans think it more prudent to abide by him than to choose another; who, though he may possibly be of higher rank, and older standing, cannot have equal experience in this particular kind of warfare.

Saint Januarius suffered martyrdom about the end of the third century. When he was beheaded, a pious lady of this city caught about an ounce of his blood, which has been carefully preserved in a bottle ever since, without having lost a single grain of its weight. This of itself, were it equally demonstrable, might be considered as a greater miracle than the circumstance on which the Neapolitans lay the whole stress, viz. that the blood which has congealed, and acquired a solid form by age, is no sooner brought near the head of the Saint, than, as a mark of veneration, it immediately liquefies. This experiment is made three different times every year, and is considered by the Neapolitans as a miracle of the first magnitude.

As the divinity of no other religion whatever is any longer attempted to be proved by fresh miracles, but all are now trusted to their own internal evidence, and to those wrought at a former period, this miracle of Saint Januarius is probably the more admired on account of its being the only one, except transubstantiation, which remains still in use, out of the vast abundance said to have been performed at various periods in support of the Roman Catholic faith. The latter is unquestionably the greater miracle, of the two; for to change a wafer into flesh and blood, is more extraordinary than to liquefy any substance whatever: Yet I once imagined the liquefaction had rather the advantage in this particular; that the change is more obvious to the senses. But I have lately been otherwise instructed, by an ingenious person, who was formerly a Jesuit. On somebody (not me, for I never do make objections in matters of faith) having observed, That it was unfortunate that the great change operated on the wafer in transubstantiation, was not visible, the person above alluded to pronounced the miracle to be much greater on that account. "For pray, Sir," said he, addressing himself to the objector, "suppose I should immediately turn that fowl, pointing to a turkey which was at that moment stalking past; suppose I should immediately turn that fowl into a woman, would you not think it very extraordinary?" "Certainly," replied the other. "Well, Sir, but after the change is actually made, and the fowl has to all intents and purposes become a woman, if it still retained the appearance of a turkey, you must acknowledge *that* would be more extraordinary still. In the same manner," continued he, "in the celebration of mass, the conversion of the wafer into the real body and blood of Jesus Christ, is a great miracle, and highly to be venerated; but, after this wonderful change has actually taken place, that the real body of Christ should, even in the eyes of the sharpest sighted spectators, still retain its original form of a wafer, is a great deal more amazing and stupendous."

But, however great a superiority the miracle of transubstantiation may have over that of St. Januarius, in the opinion of Roman Catholics in general, the Neapolitans imagine the latter is sufficient to convert infidels, and put heretics out of countenance. A zealous believer of this country, having described the miracle, breaks out into the following exclamations: "O illustre memoria! O verità irrefragabile! vengano gli Heretici, vengano, e Stupiscano, ed aprano gli occhi alla verità Cattolica, et Evangelica; Bastarebbe questo sangue di S. Gennaro sola à fare testimonia della Fede. E possibile, che a tanto, et si famoso miraculo non si converta tutta la Gentilità, ed Infedeltà alla verità Cattolica della Romana chiesa?" Though I am not such an enthusiastic admirer of the performance as this author, yet, on the other hand, I do not think that Protestants, however much they may be convinced it is a trick, have any right to call it a *clumsy trick*, without explaining in what it consists. This is a liberty which some travellers of great eminence have taken. Others have asserted, that the substance in the bottle, which is exhibited for the blood of the Saint, is something naturally solid, but which melts with a small degree of heat. When it is first brought out of the cold chapel, say those gentlemen, it is in its natural solid state; but when brought before the Saint by the priest, and rubbed between his warm hands, and breathed upon for some time, it melts; and this is the whole mystery. Though I find myself unable to explain on what principle the liquefaction depends, I am fully convinced that it must be something different from this; for I have it from the most satisfactory authority, from those who had opportunities of knowing, and who believe no more in the miracle than you do, that this congealed mass has sometimes been found in a liquid state in cold weather, before it was touched by the Priest, or brought near the head of the Saint; and that, on other occasions, it has remained solid when brought before him, notwithstanding all the efforts of the Priest to melt it. When this happens, the superstitious, which, at a very moderate calculation, comprehends ninety-nine in a hundred of the inhabitants of this city, are thrown into the utmost consternation, and are sometimes wrought up by their fears into a state of mind which is highly dangerous both to their civil and ecclesiastical governors. It is true, that this happens but seldom; for, in general, the substance in the phial, whatever it may be, is in a solid form in the chapel, and becomes liquid when brought before the Saint; but as this is not always the case, it affords reason to believe, that, whatever may have been the case when this miracle or trick, call it which you please, was first exhibited, the principle on which it depends has somehow or other been lost, and is not now understood fully even by the Priests themselves; or else they are not now so expert, as formerly, in preparing the substance which represents the Saint's blood, so as to make it remain solid when it ought, and liquefy the instant it is required.

The head and blood of the Saint are kept in a kind of press, with folding doors of silver, in the chapel of St. Januarius, belonging to the cathedral church. The real head is probably not so fresh, and well preserved, as the blood; and on that account is not exposed to the eyes of the public, but inclosed in a large silver bust, gilt and enriched with jewels of high value. This being what appears to the people, their idea of the Saint's features and complexion are taken entirely from the bust.

The blood is kept in a small repository by itself.

About mid-day, the bust, inclosing the real head, was brought with great solemnity, and placed under a kind of portico, open on all sides, that the different communities, which come in procession, may be able to traverse it, and that the people may have the comfort of beholding the miracle. The processions of that solemn day were innumerable; all the streets of Naples were crowded with the various orders of ecclesiastics, dressed in their richest robes. The monks of each convent were mustered under their own particular banners. A splendid cross was carried before each procession; and the images, in massy silver, of the Saints, peculiarly patronising the convents, followed the cross. In this order they marched from the convents to the pavilion, under which the head of St. Januarius was placed, and having done due obeisance to that great protector of this city, they marched back by a different route, in the same order, to their convent. But as there are a great many convents in Naples, and a great number of monks in each convent, though the processions began soon after mid-day, the evening was well advanced before the last of them had passed. The grand procession of all began when the others had finished. It was composed of a numerous body of clergy, and an immense multitude of people of all ranks, headed by the archbishop of Naples himself, who carried the phial containing the blood of the Saint. The D—— of H—— and I accompanied Sir W—— H—— to a house directly opposite to the portico, where the sacred head was placed. We there found a large assembly of Neapolitan nobility. A magnificent robe of velvet, richly embroidered, was thrown over the shoulders of the bust; a mitre, refulgent with jewels, was placed on its head. The archbishop, with a solemn pace, and a look full of awe and veneration, approached, holding forth the sacred phial which contained the precious lump of blood. He addressed the Saint in the humblest manner, fervently praying that he would graciously condescend to manifest his regard to his faithful votaries the people of Naples, by the usual token of ordering that lump of his sacred blood to assume its natural and original form. In those prayers he was joined by the multitude around, particularly by the women; of whom there seemed more than their proportion. My curiosity prompted me to leave the balcony, and mingle with the multitude. I got by degrees quite near the bust. Twenty minutes had already elapsed, since the archbishop had been praying with all possible earnestness, and turning the phial around and around without any effect. An old monk stood near the archbishop, and was at the utmost pains to instruct him how to handle, chafe, and rub the phial; he frequently took it into his own hands, but his manœuvres were as ineffectual as those of the archbishop. By this time the people had become exceedingly noisy; the women were quite hoarse with praying; the monk continued his operations with increased zeal; and the archbishop was all over in a profuse sweat with vexation. In whatever light the failure of the miracle might appear to others, it was a very serious matter to him; because the people consider such an event as a proof of the Saint's displeasure, and a certain indication that some dreadful calamity will ensue. This was the first opportunity he had had of officiating since his nomination to the see. There was no knowing what fancy might have entered into the heads of a superstitious populace; they might have imagined, or his enemies might have insinuated, that the failure of the miracle proceeded from St. Januarius's disapprobation of the person in whose hands it was to have taken place. I never saw more evident marks of vexation and alarm than appeared in the countenance of the right reverend personage. This alone would have convinced me that they cannot command the liquefaction when they please. While things were in this state I observed a gentleman come hastily through the crowd, and speak to the old monk, who, in a pretty loud voice, and with an accent and a grimace very expressive of chagrin, replied, "Cospetto di bacco è dura come una pietra." At the same time an acquaintance whispered me, That it would be prudent to retire, because the mob on similar occasions have been struck with a notion, that the operation of the miracle was disturbed by the presence of heretics; on which they are apt to insult them. I directly took his hint, and joined the company I had left. An universal gloom had overspread all their countenances, they talked to each other in whispers, and seemed oppressed with grief and contrition. One very beautiful young lady cried and sobbed as if her heart had been ready to break. The passions of some of the rabble without doors took a different turn; instead of sorrow, they were filled with rage and indignation at the Saint's obstinacy. They put him in mind of the zeal with which he was adored by people of all ranks in Naples; of the honours which had been conferred on him; that he was respected here more than in any other country on earth; and some went so far as to call him, an old ungrateful yellow-faced rascal, for his obduracy. It was now almost dark—and when least expected, the signal was given that the miracle was performed.—The populace filled the air with repeated shouts of joy; a band of music began to play; Te Deum was sung; couriers were dispatched to the royal family, then at Portici, with the glad tidings; the young lady dried up her tears; the countenances of our company brightened in an instant, and they sat down to cards without farther dread of eruptions, earthquakes, or pestilence.

I had remarked, during their suspence with respect to the success of the miracle, that some imputed the delay partly to the weather, which happened to be rainy, and colder than is usual at this season; and partly to the aukwardness of the Archbishop, who, never having performed before, was accused of not handling the phial in the same dexterous and efficacious manner that a person of experience would have done. While they imputed the failure to those causes, they seemed equally uneasy with the rest of the company about the consequences. It struck me that the first sentiment was perfectly inconsistent with the second. I mentioned this to a French gentleman, who is here as travelling companion to the young Comte de G——. "If," said I, "the weather, or the unskilfulness of the Archbishop, has prevented the substance in the phial from becoming liquid, this surely cannot be an indication that Heaven or the Saint is displeased; if, on the contrary, the blood continuing solid in the presence of the Saint, proceeds from Heaven or the Saint being offended, then no kind of weather, and no kind of expertness on the part of the Archbishop, could have rendered it liquid."—"Monsieur," said he, "voilà ce qu'on appelle raisonner, ce que ces messieurs ne font jamais."

The same evening, an acquaintance of mine, who is also a Roman Catholic, and who remained close by the Archbishop till all was over, assured me, that the miracle had failed entirely; for the old monk seeing no symptom of the blood liquefying, had called out that the miracle had succeeded; on which the signal had been given, the people had shouted, the Archbishop had held up the bottle, moving it with a rapid motion before the eyes of the spectators, and nobody chusing to contradict what every body wished, he had been allowed to cover up the phial, and carry it back to the Chapel, with the contents, in the same form they had come abroad. How far this account is exactly true, I will not take on me to assert; I was not near enough to see the transaction myself, and I have only the authority of this person, having heard no other body say they had observed the same.

LETTER LXV.

The tomb of Virgil is on the mountain of Pausilippo, a little above the grotto of that name; you ascend to it by a narrow path which runs through a vineyard; it is overgrown with ivy leaves and shaded with branches, shrubs, and bushes; an ancient bay-tree, with infinite propriety, overhangs it. Many a solitary walk have I taken to this place. The earth, which contains his ashes, we expect to find clothed in the brightest verdure. Viewed from the magic spot, the objects which adorn the bay become doubly interesting. The Poet's verses are here recollected with additional pleasure; the verses of Virgil are interwoven in our minds with a thousand interesting ideas, with the memory of our boyish years, or the sportive scenes of childhood, of our earliest friends and companions, many of whom are now dead; and those who still live, and for whom we retain the first impression of affection, are at such a distance as renders the hopes of seeing them again very uncertain. No wonder, therefore, when in a contemplative mood, that our steps are often directed to a spot so well calculated to create and cherish sentiments congenial with the state of our mind. But then comes an antiquarian, who, with his odious doubts, disturbs the pleasing source of our enjoyment; and from the fair and delightful fields of fancy, conveys us in a moment to a dark, barren, and comfortless desert;—he *doubts*, whether this be the real place where the ashes of Virgil were deposited; and tells us an unsatisfactory story about the other side of the bay, and that he is rather inclined to believe that the Poet was buried somewhere there, without fixing on any particular spot.

Would to heaven those doubters would keep their minds to themselves, and not ruffle the tranquillity of believers!

But, after all, why should not this be the real tomb of Virgil? Why should the enthusiasts, who delight in pilgrimages to this spot, be deprived of that pleasure? Why should the Poet's ghost be allowed to wander along the dreary banks of Styx, till the antiquarians erect a cenotaph in his honour? Even they acknowledge that he was buried on this bay, and near Naples; and tradition has fixed on this spot, which, exclusive of other presumptions, is a much stronger evidence in its favour than their vague conjectures against it.

In your way to the classic fields of Baia and Cumæ, you pass through the grotto of Pausilippo, a subterraneous passage through the mountain, near a mile in length, about twenty feet in breadth, and thirty or forty in height, every where, except at the two extremities, where it is much higher. People of fashion generally drive through this passage with torches, but the country people and foot passengers find their way without much difficulty by the light which enters at the extremities, and at two holes pierced through the mountain near the middle of the grotto, which admit light from above.

Mr. Addison tells us, that the common people of Naples in his time believed that this passage through the mountain was the work of magic, and that Virgil was the magician. But this is the age of scepticism; and the common people, in imitation of people of fashion, begin to harbour doubts concerning all their old established opinions. A Neapolitan Valet-de-place asked an English gentleman lately, Whether Signior Virgilio, of whom he had heard so much, had really, and bona fide, been a magician or not? "A magician," replied the Englishman; "ay, that he was, and a very great magician too." "And do you," resumed the Valet, "believe it was he who pierced this rock?" "As for this particular rock," answered the Master, "I will not swear to it from my own knowledge, because it was done before I was born; but I am ready to make oath, that I have known him pierce, and even melt, some very obdurate substances."

Two miles beyond the Grotta di Pausilippe, is a circular lake, about half a mile in diameter, called Lago d'Agnano; on whose margin is situated the famous Grotta del Cane, where so many dogs have been tortured and suffocated, to shew the effect of a vapour which rises about a foot above the bottom of this little cave, and is destructive of animal life. A dog having his head held in this vapour, is convulsed in a few minutes, and soon after falls to the earth motionless. This experiment is repeated for the amusement of every unfeeling person, who has half a crown in his pocket, and affects a turn for natural philosophy. The experiment is commonly made on dogs; because they, of all animals, show the greatest affection for man, and prefer his company to that of their own species, or of any other living creature. The fellows who attend at this cave have always some miserable dogs, with ropes about their necks, ready for this cruel purpose. If the poor animals were unconscious of what was to happen, it would be less affecting; but they struggle to get free, and show every symptom of horror when they are dragged to this cave of torment. I should have been happy to have taken the effect of the vapour for granted, without a new trial; but some of the company were of a more philosophical turn of mind than I have any pretensions to. When the unhappy animal found all his efforts to escape were ineffectual, he seemed to plead for mercy by the dumb eloquence of looks, and the blandishments natural to his species. While he licked the hand of his keeper, the unrelenting wretch dashed him a blow, and thrust his head into the murderous vapour.

When the real utility of the knowledge acquired by cruel experiments on animals (a practice which has been carried to dreadful lengths of late) is fairly stated, and compared with the exquisiteness of *their* sufferings, the benefit resulting to mankind from thence will seem too dearly bought in the eyes of a person of humanity. Humanity! If language had belonged to other animals besides man, might not they have chosen that word to express—cruelty? if they had, thank God, they would have done injustice to many of the human race. I have left the poor dog too long in the vapour; much longer than he remained in reality. The D—— of H——, shocked at the fellow's barbarity, wrested the dog from his hands, bore him to the open air, and gave him life and liberty; which he seemed to enjoy with all the bounding rapture of gladness and gratitude. If you should ever come this way, pray do not insist on seeing the experiment; it is not worth while; the thing is ascertained; it is beyond a doubt that this vapour convulses and kills every breathing animal.

You come next to the favourite fields of fancy and poetical fiction. The Campi Phlegrei, where Jupiter overcame the giants; the solfaterra still smoking, as if from the effects of his thunder; the Monte Nova, which was thrown suddenly from the bowels of the earth, as if the sons of Titan had intended to renew the war; the Monte Barbaro, formerly Mons Gaurus, the favourite of Bacchus; the grotto of the Cumæan Sibyl; the noxious and gloomy lakes of Avernus and Acheron; and the green bowers of Elysium.

The town of Puzzoli, and its environs, present such a number of objects, worthy of the attention of the antiquarian, the natural philosopher, and the classic scholar, that to describe all with the minuteness they deserve, would fill volumes.

The Temple of Jupiter Serapis at Puzzoli, is accounted a very interesting monument of antiquity; being quite different from the Roman and Greek temples, and built in the manner of the Asiatics, probably by the Egyptian and Asiatic merchants settled at Puzzoli, which was the great emporium of Italy, until the Romans built Ostia and Antium.

Sylla having abdicated the Dictatorship, retired, and passed the remainder of his life in this city.

The ruins of Cicero's villa, near this city, are of such extent, as to give a high idea of the wealth of this great orator. Had Fortune always bestowed her gifts with so much propriety, she never would have been accused of blindness. When the truly great are blessed with riches, it affords pleasure to every candid mind. Neither this villa near Puzzoli, that at Tusculum, nor any of his other country-seats, were the scenes of idleness or riot. They are distinguished by the names of the works he composed there; works which have always been the delight of the learned, and which, still more than the important services he rendered his country when in office, have contributed to immortalize his name.

The bay between Puzzoli and Baia is about a league in breadth. In crossing this in a boat, you see the ruins called Ponte di Caligula, from their being thought the remains of a bridge which Caligula attempted to build across. They are by others, with more probability, thought to be the ruins of a mole built with arches. Having passed over this gulph, a new field of curiosities presents itself. The baths and prisons of Nero, the tomb of Agrippina, the temples of Venus, of Diana, and of Mercury, and the ruins of the ancient city of Cumæ; but no vestiges now remain of many of those magnificent villas which adorned this luxurious coast, nor even of the town of Baia. The whole of this beauteous bay, formerly the seat of pleasure, and, at one period, the most populous spot in Italy, is now very thinly inhabited; and the contrast is still stronger between the antient opulence and present poverty, than between the numbers of its antient and present inhabitants. It must be acknowledged, that we can hardly look around us, in any part of this world, without perceiving objects which, to a contemplative mind, convey reflections on the instability of grandeur, and the sad vicissitudes and reverses to which human affairs are liable; but *here* those objects are so numerous, and so striking, that they must make an impression on the most careless passenger.

LETTER LXVI.

Naples.

As the Court are not at present at Casserta, we have not seen that place in all its splendour; we passed, however, one very agreeable day there, with Lady H—— and S—H—— F——n.

The palace at Casserta was begun in the year 1750, after a plan of Vanvitelli; the work is now carried on under the direction of his son. While the present King of Spain remained at Naples, there were generally about two thousand workmen employed; at present there are about five hundred. It will be finished in a few years, and will then, unquestionably, be one of the most spacious and magnificent palaces in Europe. It has been said, that London is too large a capital for the island of Great Britain; and it has been compared to a turgid head placed on an emaciated body. The palace of Casserta also seems out of proportion with the revenues of this kingdom. It is not, properly speaking, a head too large for the body; but rather an ornament, by much too expensive and bulky for either head or body. This palace is situated about sixteen miles north from Naples, on the plain where ancient Capua stood. It was thought prudent to found a building, on which such sums of money were to be lavished, at a considerable distance from Mount Vesuvius. It were to be wished, that the contents of the cabinet at Portici were removed from the same dangerous neighbourhood. That he might not be limited in ground for the gardens, may have been his Spanish Majesty's motive for choosing that his palace should be at a distance from Naples; and that it might not be exposed to insult from an enemy's fleet, was probably the reason that determined him to place it at a distance from the sea.

This immense building is of a rectangular form, seven hundred and fifty feet English, by five hundred and eighty; about one hundred and twelve feet high, comprehending five habitable stories, which contain such a number of apartments as will accommodate the most numerous court, without any accessary buildings.

The rectangle is divided into four courts, each of about two hundred and fifty-two feet by one hundred and seventy. In each of the two principal fronts, are three corresponding gates, forming three openings, which pierce the whole building. The middle gate forms the entry to a magnificent portico, through which the coaches drive. In the middle of this, and in the centre of the edifice, there is a vestibule of an octogonal form, which opens into the four grand courts at four sides of the octogon; two other sides open into the portico, one to the staircase; and, at the eighth side, there is a statue of Hercules, crowned by Victory, with this inscription,

VIRTUS POST FORTIA FACTA CORONAT.

The grand staircase is adorned with the richest marble; the upper vestibule to which you ascend by this noble stair, is an octogon also, and surrounded by twenty-four pillars of yellow marble, each of which is of one piece of eighteen feet high, without including the pedestal or capital. From this upper vestibule there are entries into—But I have a notion you are tired of this description, which I assure you is likewise my case. I beg, therefore, you may take it for granted, that the apartments within, particularly their Majesties, and that destined for balls and theatrical entertainments, correspond with the magnificence of the external appearance.

Among the workmen employed in finishing this palace and the gardens, there are one hundred and fifty Africans; for as the King of Naples is constantly at war with the Barbary States, he always has a number of their sailors prisoners, all of whom are immediately employed as slaves in the gallies, or at some public work. There are at present at Casserta, about the same number of Christian slaves; all of these have been condemned to this servitude for some crime, some of them for the greatest of all crimes; they are, however, better clothed and fed than the Africans. This is done, no doubt, in honour of the Christian religion, and to demonstrate that Christians, even after they have been found guilty of the blackest crimes, are worthier men, and more deserving of lenity, than Mahometan prisoners, however innocent they may be in all *other* respects.

The gardens belonging to this palace are equally extensive and magnificent. A great number of fine statues, most of them copies of the best antique, are kept in a storehouse till the gardens are finished, when they will be placed in them. The largest and finest elephant I ever saw is here at present; he is kept by African slaves: they seem to know how to manage him perfectly; he is well thriven, and goes through a number of tricks and evolutions with much docility and judgment.

In the garden, there is an artificial water and island. This, if one may venture to say so, seems a little injudicious; it brings to our memory the bay of Naples, with its islands, a recollection by no means favourable to this royal contrivance. In this island there is a kind of a castle, regularly fortified, with a ditch around it, and ramparts, bastions, sally-ports, &c. &c. and a numerous train of artillery, some of them nine or ten *ouncers*. I no sooner entered this fort, than I wished that Uncle Toby and Corporal Trim had been of our party; it would have charmed the soul of the worthy veteran and his faithful servant.

I asked the man who attended us, What he imagined this fortification was intended for?—Sir H—— F—— said, "The cannon were certainly designed against the frogs, who were continually attempting to scale the ramparts from the ditch."—I asked again, What was the real design of erecting this fort? The man answered, stretching out his arms, and making as wide a circle with them as he could, "Tutto, tutto per il sollazo del Re." "Yes," said I, "it is surely in the highest degree reasonable, that not only this fort, but the whole kingdom, should be appropriated to the amusement of his Majesty."— "Certo," replied the man. I wished to see how far the fellow's liberality would go—"Not only this kingdom," continued I, "but all Europe would be highly honoured in contributing to the amusement of his Majesty." "Certo, certo," said the man.

LETTER LXVII.

The King and Queen lately paid a visit to four of the principal nunneries in this town. Their motive was, to gratify the curiosity of the Archduchess, and her husband, Prince Albert of Saxony. I ought to have informed you, that this illustrious couple left Vienna some months after us, with an intention to make the tour of Italy. We had the honour of seeing them frequently while at Rome, where they conciliated the affections of the Italian nobles by their obliging manners, as much as they commanded respect by their high rank. The Archduchess is a very beautiful woman, and more distinguished by the propriety of her conduct, than by either birth or beauty. As white, by the link of contrast, is connected with the idea of black; so this amiable Duchess sometimes recals those to people's memories, whose ideas of dignity are strongly contrasted with hers. Conscious, from her infancy, of the highest rank, and accustomed to honours, it never enters into her thoughts that any person will fail in paying her a due respect; while they, eternally jealous that enough of respect is not paid them, give themselves airs which would be intolerable in an Empress. A smile of benignity puts all who approach this Princess perfectly at their ease, and dignity sits as smoothly on her as a well-made garment; while, on them, it bristles out like the quills of a porcupine, or the feathers of an enraged turkey-cock.

As nobody is permitted to enter those convents, except on such extraordinary occasions as this, when they are visited by the Sovereigns, the British Minister seized this opportunity of procuring an order for admitting the D—— of H—— and me. We accordingly accompanied him, and a few others, who were in the King's suite. I have seen various nunneries in different parts of Europe, but none that could be compared even with the meanest of those four in this city, for neatness and conveniency. Each of them is provided with a beautiful garden; and the situation of one is the happiest that can be imagined, commanding a prospect nearly as extensive as that from the Carthusian convent near the castle of St. Elmo. Those four nunneries are for the reception of young ladies of good families; and, into one in particular, none but such as are of very high rank can be admitted, either as pensioners, or to take the veil. Each of the young ladies in this splendid convent, have both a summer and a winter apartment, and many other accommodations unknown in other retreats of this nature. The royal visitors were received in all of them by the Lady Abbess, at the head of the oldest of the sisterhood; they were afterwards presented with nosegays, and served with fruit, sweetmeats, and a variety of cooling drinks, by the younger nuns. The Queen and her amiable sister received all very graciously;

conversing familiarly with the Lady Abbesses, and asking a few obliging questions of each.

In one convent the company were surprised, on being led into a large parlour, to find a table covered, and every appearance of a most plentiful cold repast, consisting of several joints of meat, hams, fowl, fish, and various other dishes. It seemed rather ill-judged to have prepared a feast of such a solid nature immediately after dinner; for those royal visits were made in the afternoon. The Lady Abbess, however, earnestly pressed their Majesties to sit down, with which they complied, and their example was followed by the Archduchess and some of the ladies; the nuns stood behind, to serve their Royal guests. The Queen chose a slice of cold turkey, which, on being cut up, turned out a large piece of lemon ice, of the shape and appearance of a roasted turkey. All the other dishes were ices of various kinds, disguised under the forms of joints of meat, fish, and fowl, as above mentioned. The gaiety and good humour of the King, the affable and engaging behaviour of the Royal sisters, and the satisfaction which beamed from the plump countenance of the Lady Abbess, threw an air of cheerfulness on this scene; which was interrupted, however, by gleams of melancholy reflection, which failed not to dart across the mind, at sight of so many victims to the pride of family, to avarice, and superstition. Many of those victims were in the full bloom of health and youth, and some of them were remarkably handsome. There is something in a nun's dress which renders the beauty of a young woman more interesting than is in the power of the gayest, richest, and most laboured ornaments. This certainly does not proceed from any thing remarkably becoming in black and white flannel. The Lady Abbess and the elderly nuns made no more impression in their vestal robes, than those stale, forlorn dames, whom you may see displaying their family jewels and shrivelled countenances every night at Ranelagh or in the side-boxes. The interest you take in a beautiful woman is heightened on seeing her in the dress of a nun, by the opposition which you imagine exists between the life to which her rash vows have condemned her, and that to which her own unbiassed inclination would have led her. You are moved with pity, which you know is a-kin to love, on seeing a young blooming creature doomed to retirement and self-denial, who was formed by nature for society and enjoyment.

If we may credit the ancient poets, those young women who are confined to a cloister life on any part of this coast, are more to be pitied than they would be under the same restraint elsewhere. They tell us, the very air in this part of Italy is repugnant to that kind of constitution, and that turn of mind, of which it would be peculiarly happy for nuns to be possessed. Propertius intreats his Cynthia not to remain too long on a shore which he seems to think dangerous to the chastest maiden.

Tu modo quamprimum corruptas desere Baias—

...

Littora quæ fuerant castis inimica puellis.

Martial asserts, that a woman who came hither as chaste as Penelope, if she remained any time, would depart as licentious and depraved as Helen,

Penelope venit, abit Helene.

I have certainly met with ladies, after they had resided some time at Naples, who, in point of character and constitution, were thought to have a much stronger resemblance to Helen than to Penelope; but as I have no great faith in the sudden operation of physical causes in matters of this kind, I never doubted of those ladies having carried the same disposition to Naples that they brought from it. Though there are not wanting those who affirm, that the influence of this seducing climate is evident *now* in as strong a degree as it is described to have been anciently; that it pervades people of all ranks and conditions, and that in the convents themselves;

Even there where frozen chastity retires,

Love finds an altar for forbidden fires.

Others, who carry their researches still deeper, and pretend to have a distinct knowledge of the effect of aliment through all its changes on the human constitution, think, that the amorous disposition, imputed to Neapolitans, is only in part owing to their voluptuous climate, but in a far greater degree to the hot, sulphureous nature of their soil, which those profound naturalists declare communicates its fiery qualities to the juices of vegetables; thence they are conveyed to the animals who feed on them, and particularly to man, whose nourishment consisting both of animal and vegetable food, he must have in his veins a double dose of the stimulating particles in question. No wonder, therefore, say those nice investigators of cause and effect, that the inhabitants of this country are more given to amorous indulgencies, than those who are favoured with a chaster soil and a colder climate.

For my own part, I must acknowledge, that I have seen nothing, since I came to Naples, to justify the general imputations above mentioned, or to support this very ingenious theory. On the contrary, there are circumstances from which the opposers of this system draw very different conclusions; for every system of philosophy, like every Minister of Great Britain, has an opposition. The gentlemen in opposition to the voluptuous influence of this climate, and the fiery effects of this soil, undermine the foundation of their antagonists' theory, by asserting, that, so far from being of a warmer complexion than their neighbours, the Neapolitans are of colder constitutions, or more philosophic in the command of their passions, than any people in Europe. Do not the lower class of men, say they, strip themselves before the houses which front the bay, and bathe in the sea without the smallest ceremony? Are not numbers of those stout, athletic figures, during the heat of the day, seen walking and sporting on the shore perfectly naked; and with no more idea of shame, than Adam felt in his state of innocence; while the ladies from their coaches, and the servant-maids and young girls, who pass along, contemplate this singular spectacle with as little apparent emotion as the ladies in Hyde Park behold a review of the horse-guards?

As Sir W—— and L——y H—— are preparing to visit England, and the D—— feels no inclination to remain after they are gone, we intend to return to Rome in a few days.

LETTER LXVIII.

We delayed visiting Tivoli, Frescati, and Albano, till our return from Naples.

The Campagna is an uninhabited plain, surrounding the city of Rome, bounded on one side by the sea, and on the other by an amphitheatre of hills, crowned with towns, villages, and villas, which form the finest landscapes that can be imagined. The ancient Romans were wont to seek shelter from the scorching heats of summer, among the woods and lakes of those hills; and the Cardinals and Roman Princes, at the same season, retire to their villas; while many of the wealthier sort of citizens take lodgings in the villages, during the season of gathering the vines.

On the road from Rome to Tivoli, about three miles from the latter, strangers are desired to visit a kind of lake called Solfatara formerly Lakus Albulus, and there shown certain substances, to which they give the name of Floating Islands. They are nothing else than bunches of bullrushes, springing from a thin soil, formed by dust and sand blown from the adjacent ground, and glued together by the bitumen which swims on the surface of this lake, and the sulphur with which its waters are impregnated. Some of these islands are twelve or fifteen yards in length; the soil is sufficiently strong to bear five or six people, who, by the means of a pole, may move to different parts of the lake, as if they were in a boat. This lake empties itself, by a whitish, muddy stream, into the Teverone, the ancient Anio; a vapour, of a sulphureous smell, arising from it as it flows. The ground near this rivulet, as also around the borders of the lake, resounds, as if it were hollow, when a horse gallops over it. The water of this lake has the singular quality of covering every substance which it touches with a hard, white, stoney matter. On throwing a bundle of small sticks or shrubs into it, they will, in a few days, be covered with a white crust; but, what seems still more extraordinary, this encrusting quality is not so strong in the lake itself, as in the canal, or little rivulet that runs from it; and the farther the water has flowed from the lake, till it is quite lost in the Anio, the stronger this quality is. Those small, round encrustations, which cover the sand and pebbles, resembling sugar-plums, are called Confetti di Tivoli. Fishes are found in the Anio, both above and below Tivoli, till it receives the Albula; after which, during the rest of its course to the Tiber, there are none. The waters of this lake had a high medical reputation anciently, but they are in no esteem at present.

Near the bottom of the eminence on which Tivoli stands, are the ruins of the vast and magnificent villa built by the emperor Adrian. In this were comprehended an amphitheatre, several temples, a library, a circus, a naumachia. The emperor also gave to the buildings and gardens of this famous villa the names of the most celebrated places; as the Academia, the Lycæum, the Prytaneum of Athens, the Tempe of Thessaly, and the Elysian fields and infernal regions of the poets. There were also commodious apartments for a vast number of guests, all admirably distributed with baths, and every conveniency. Every quarter of the world contributed to ornament this famous villa, whose spoils have since formed the principal ornaments of the Campidoglio, the Vatican, and the palaces of the Roman Princes. It is said to have been three miles in length, and above a mile in breadth. Some antiquarians make it much larger; but the ruins, now remaining, do not mark a surface of a quarter of that extent.

At no great distance, they shew the place to which the Eastern Queen Zenobia was confined, after she was brought in triumph to Rome by the emperor Aurelian.

The town of Tivoli is now wretchedly poor; it boasts however greater antiquity than Rome itself, being the ancient Tibur, which, Horace informs us, was founded by a Grecian colony.

Tibur Argæo positum colono

Sit meæ sedes utinam senectæ.

Ovid gives it the same origin, in the fourth book of the Fasti.

——Jam mœnia Tiburis udi

Stabant; Argolicæ quod posuere manus.

This was a populous and flourishing town in remoter antiquity; but it appears to have been thinly inhabited in the reign of Augustus. Horace, in an Epistle to Mæcenas, says,

Parvum parva decent. Mihi jam non Regia Roma,

Sed *vacuum Tibur* placet——

Though the town itself was not populous, the beauty of the situation, and wholesomeness of the air, prompted great numbers of illustrious Romans, both before the final destruction of the Republic, and afterwards in Augustus's time, to build country-houses in the neighbourhood. Julius Cæsar had a villa here, which he was under the necessity of selling to defray the expence of the public shews and games he exhibited to the people during his Ædileship. Plutarch says, that his liberality and magnificence, on this occasion, obscured the glory of all who had preceded him in the office, and gained the hearts of the people to such a degree, that they were ready to invent new offices and new honours for him. He then laid the foundation of that power and popularity, which enabled him, in the end, to overturn the constitution of his country. Caius Cassius had also a country house here; where Marcus Brutus and he are said to have had frequent meetings, and to have formed the plan which terminated the ambition of Cæsar, and again offered to Rome that freedom which she had not the virtue to accept. Here, also, was the villa of Augustus, whose success in life arose at the field of Philippi from which he fled, was confirmed by the death of the most virtuous citizens of Rome, and who, without the talents, reaped the fruits of the labours and vast projects of Julius. Lepidus the Triumvir, Cæcilius Metellus, Quintilius Varus, the poets Catullus and Propertius, and other distinguished Romans, had villas in this town or its environs; and you are shewn the spots on which they stood; but nothing renders Tibur so interesting, as the frequent mention which Horace makes of it in his writings. His great patron and friend Mæcenas had a villa here, the ruins of which are to be seen on the south bank of the Anio; and it was pretty generally supposed, that the poet's own house and farm were very near it, and immediately without the walls of Tibur; but it has been of late asserted, with great probability, that Horace's farm was situated nine miles above that of Mæcenas's, at the side of a stream called Licenza, formerly Digentia, near the hill Lucretilis, in the country of the ancient Sabines. Those who hold this opinion say, that when Horace talks of Tibur, he alludes to the villa of Mæcenas; but when he mentions Digentia, or Lucretilis, his own house and farm are to be understood; as in the eighteenth Epistle of the first book,

Me quoties resicit gelidus Digentia rivus,

Quem Mandela bibit, rugosus frigore pagus;

Quid sentire putas, quid credis, amice, precari?

the seventeenth Ode of the first book,

Velox amænum sæpe Lucretilem

Mutat Lycæo Faunus;——

and in other passages. But whether the poet's house and farm were near the town of Tibur, or at a distance from it, his writings sufficiently show that he spent much of his time there; and it is probable that he composed great part of his works in that favourite retreat. This he himself in some measure declares, in that fine Ode addressed to Julius Antonius, son of Mark Antony, by Fulvia; the same whom Augustus first pardoned, and afterwards put privately to death, on account of an intrigue into which Antonius was seduced by the abandoned Julia, daughter of Augustus.

———Ego, apis Matinæ

More modoque,

Grata carpentis thyma per laborem

Plurimum, circa nemus uvidique

Tiburis ripas, operosa parvus

Carmina fingo.

If you ever come to Tivoli, let it not be with a numerous party; come alone, or with a single friend, and be sure to put your Horace in your pocket. You will read him here with more enthusiasm than elsewhere; you will imagine you see the philosophic poet wandering among the groves, sometimes calmly meditating his moral precepts, and sometimes *his eye in a fine frenzy* rolling with all the fire of poetic enthusiasm. If Tivoli had nothing else to recommend it but its being so often sung by the most elegant of the poets, and its having been the residence of so many illustrious men, these circumstances alone would render it worthy the attention of travellers; but it will also be interesting to many on account of its cascade, the Sibyl's Temple, and the Villa Estense.

The river Anio, deriving its source from a part of the Apennines, fifty miles above Tivoli, glides through a plain till it comes near that town, when it is confined for a short space between two hills, covered with groves. These were supposed to have been the residence of the Sibyl Albunea, to whom the temple was dedicated. The river, moving with augmented rapidity as its channel is confined, at length rushes headlong over a lofty precipice; the noise of its fall resounds through the hills and groves of Tivoli; a liquid cloud arises from the foaming water, which afterwards divides into numberless small cascades, waters several orchards, and, having gained the plain, flows quietly for the rest of its course, till it loses itself in the Tiber. It is not surprising that the following lines have been so often quoted by those who visit the Sibyl's Temple, because they delineate, in the most expressive manner, some of the principal features of the country around it,

Me nec tam patiens Lacedæmon,

Nec tam Larissæ percussit campus opimæ,

Quam domus Albuneæ resonantis,

Et præceps Anio, et Tiburni lucus, et uda

Mobilibus pomaria rivis.

The elegant and graceful form of the beautiful little temple I have so often mentioned, indicates its having been built when the arts were in the highest state of perfection at Rome. Its proportions are not more happy than its situation, on a point of the mountain fronting the great cascade.

Before they take their leave of Tivoli, strangers usually visit the Villa Estense, belonging to the Duke of Modena. It was built by Hippolitus of Este, Cardinal of Ferrara, and brother to the duke of that name; but more distinguished by being the person to whom Ariosto addressed his Poem of Orlando Furioso. The house itself is not in the finest style of architecture. There are many whimsical waterworks in the gardens. Those who do not approve of the taste of their construction, still owe them some degree of respect, on account of their being the first grand waterworks in Europe; much more ancient than those of Versailles. The situation is noble, the terraces lofty, the trees large and venerable; and though the ground is not laid out to the greatest advantage, yet the whole has a striking air of magnificence and grandeur.

LETTER LXIX.

Frescati is an agreeable village, on the declivity of a hill, about twelve miles from Rome. It derives its name from the coolness of the air, and *fresh* verdure of the fields around. It is a bishop's see, and always possessed by one of the six eldest Cardinals. At present it belongs to the Cardinal Duke of York, who, whether in the country or at Rome, passes the greatest part of his time in the duties and ceremonies of a religion, of whose truth he seems to have the fullest conviction; and who, living himself in great simplicity, and not in the usual style of Cardinals, spends a large proportion of his revenue in acts of charity and benevolence; *the world forgetting, by the world forgot*, except by those who enjoy the comforts of life through his bounty.

Tivoli was the favourite residence of the ancient Romans. The moderns give the preference to Frescati, in whose neighbourhood some of the most magnificent villas in Italy are situated.

The villa Aldobrandini, called also Belvedere, is the most remarkable, on account of its fine situation, extensive gardens, airy terraces, its grottos, cascades, and waterworks. Over a saloon, near the grand cascade, is the following inscription:

HUC EGO MIGRAVI MUSIS COMITATUS APOLLO,
HIC DELPHI, HIC HELICON, HIC MIHI DELOS ERIT.

The walls are adorned with a representation of Apollo and the Muses; and some of that God's adventures are painted in Fresco by Domenichino, particularly the manner in which he treated Marsyas. This, in my humble opinion, had better been omitted; both because it is a disagreeable subject for a picture, and because it does no honour to Apollo. Marsyas unquestionably was an object of contempt and ridicule, on account of his presumption; but the punishment said to have been inflicted on him exceeds all bounds, and renders the inflictor more detestable in our eyes than the insolent satyr himself. This story is so very much out of character, and so unlike the elegant god of poetry and music, that I am inclined to suspect it is not true. There is a report, equally incredible, which has been propagated by malicious people concerning his sister Diana; I do not mean her rencounter with Actæon, for the Goddess of Chastity may, without inconsistency, be supposed cruel, but it is quite impossible to reconcile her general character with the stories of her nocturnal visits to Endymion.

The villa Ludovisi is remarkable for its gardens and waterworks. The hills on which Frescati is situated, afford great abundance of water, a circumstance of which the owners of those villas have profited, all of them being ornamented with fountains, cascades, or waterworks of some kind or other.

The villa Taverna, belonging to the Prince Borghese, is one of the finest and best furnished of any in the neighbourhood of Rome. From this you ascend through gardens to Monte Dracone, another palace on a more lofty situation, belonging also to that Prince, and deriving its name from the arms of his family. The ancient city of Tusculum is supposed to have stood on the spot, or very near it, where Frescati now is built; and at the distance of about a mile and a half, it is generally believed, was the Tusculan villa of Cicero, at a place now called Grotta Ferrata. Some Greek monks of the order of St. Basil, flying from the persecution of the Saracens in the eleventh century, were permitted to build a convent on the ruins of Cicero's famous house. They still perform the service in the Greek language.

Whichever way you walk from Frescati, you have the most delightful scenes before you. I passed two very agreeable days, wandering through the gardens and from villa to villa. The pleasure of our party was not a little augmented by the observations of Mr. B——, a lively old gentleman from Scotland, a man of worth but no antiquarian, and indeed no admirer of any thing, ancient or modern, which has not some relation to his native country; but to ballance that indifference, he feels the warmest regard for every thing which has. We extended our walks as far as the lake of Nemi, a bason of water lying in a very deep bottom, about four miles in circumference, whose surrounding hills are covered with tall and shady trees. Here

> Black Melancholy sits, and round her throws
>
> A death-like silence, and a dread repose;
>
> Her gloomy presence saddens all the scene,
>
> Shades every flower, and darkens every green.

I never saw a place more formed for contemplation and solemn ideas. In ancient times there was a temple here sacred to Diana. The lake itself was called Speculum Dianæ, and Lacus Triviæ, and is the place mentioned in the seventh Book of the Æneid, where the Fury Alecto is described blowing the trumpet of war, at whose dreadful sound the woods and mountains shook, and mothers, trembling for their children, pressed them to their bosoms.

> Contremuit nemus, et sylvæ intonuere profundæ,

Audiit et triviæ longe lacus———[7]

Et trepidæ matres pressere ad pectora natus.

We returned by Gensano, Marino, La Riccia, and Castel Gondolfo. All the villages and villas I have named communicate with each other by fine walks and avenues of lofty trees, whose intermingling branches form a continued shade for the traveller. Castel Gondolfo is a little village near the lake Albano, on one extremity of which is a castle, belonging to his Holiness, from which the village takes its name; there is nothing remarkably fine in this villa, except its situation. Near the village of Castel Gondolfo, is the villa Barbarini, within the gardens of which are the ruins of an immense palace, built by the Emperor Domitian. There is a charming walk, about a mile in length, along the side of the lake from Castel Gondolfo to the town of Albano. The lake of Albano is an oval piece of water of about seven or eight miles circumference, whose margin is finely adorned with groves and trees of various verdure, beautifully reflected from the transparent bosom of the lake; and which, with the surrounding hills, and the Castel Gondolfo which crowns one of them, has a fine picturesque effect.

The grand scale on which the beauties of nature appear in Switzerland and the Alps, has been considered by some, as too vast for the pencil; but among the sweet hills and vallies of Italy, her features are brought nearer the eye, are fully seen and understood, and appear in all the bloom of rural loveliness. Tivoli, Albano, and Frescati, therefore, are the favourite abodes of the landscape-painters who travel to this country for improvement; and in the opinion of some, those delightful villages furnish studies better suited to the powers of their art, than even Switzerland itself. Nothing can surpass the admirable assemblage of hills, meadows, lakes, cascades, gardens, ruins, groves, and terraces, which charm the eye, as you wander among the shades of Frescati and Albano, which appear in new beauty as they are viewed from different points, and captivate the beholder with endless variety. One reflection obtrudes itself on the mind, and disturbs the satisfaction which such pleasing scenes would otherwise produce; it arises from beholding the poverty of infinitely the greater part of the inhabitants of those villages— Not that they seem miserable or discontented—a few roasted chesnuts, and some bunches of grapes, which they may have for a penny, will maintain them; but the easier they are satisfied, and the less repining they are, the more earnestly do we wish that they were better provided for. Good heavens! why should so much be heaped on a few, whom profusion cannot satisfy; while a bare competency is withheld from multitudes, whom penury cannot render discontented?

The most commanding view is from the garden of a convent of Capucins, at no great distance from Albano. Directly before you is the lake, with the mountains and woods which surround it, and the castle of Gondolfo; on one hand is Frescati with all its villas; on the other, the towns of Albano, La Riccia, and Gensano; beyond these you have an uninterrupted view of the Campagna, with St. Peter's church and the city of Rome in the middle; the whole prospect being bounded by the hills of Tivoli, the Apennines, and the Mediterranean.

While we contemplated all these objects with pleasure and admiration, an English gentleman of the party said to Mr. B——, "There is not a prospect equal to this in all France or Germany, and not any superior even in England." "That I well believe," replied the Caledonian; "but if I had you in Scotland, I could shew you several with which this is by no means to be compared." "Indeed! Pray in what part of Scotland are they to be seen?" "I presume you never was at the castle of Edinburgh, Sir?" "Never." "Or at Stirling?" "Never." "Did you ever see Loch Lomond, Sir?" "I never did." "I suppose I need not ask, whether you have ever been in Aberdeenshire, or the Highlands, or—" "I must confess once for all," interrupted the Englishman, "that I have the misfortune never to have seen any part of Scotland." "Then I am not surprised," said the Scot, taking a large pinch of snuff, "that you think this the finest view you ever saw." "I presume you think those in Scotland a great deal finer?" "A very great deal indeed, Sir; why that lake, for example, is a pretty thing enough; I dare swear, many an English nobleman would give a good deal to have such another before his house; but Loch Lomond is thirty miles in length, Sir! there are above twenty islands in it, Sir! that is a lake for you. As for their desert of a Campagna, as they call it, no man who has eyes in his head, Sir, will compare it to the fertile valley of Stirling, with the Forth, the most beautiful river in Europe, twining through it." "Do you really in your conscience imagine," said the Englishman, "that the Forth is a finer river than the Thames?" "The Thames!" exclaimed the North Briton, "Why, my dear Sir, the Thames at London is a mere gutter, in comparison of the Firth of Forth at Edinburgh." "I suppose then," said the Englishman, recovering himself, "you do not approve of the view from Windsor Castle?" "I ask your pardon," replied the other; "I approve of it very much; it is an exceeding pretty kind of a prospect; the country appears from it as agreeable to the sight as any plain flat country, crowded with trees, and intersected by enclosures, can well do; but I own I am of opinion, that mere fertile fields, woods, rivers, and meadows, can never, of themselves, perfectly satisfy the eye." "You imagine, no doubt," said the Englishman, "that a few heath-covered mountains and rocks embellish a country very much?" "I am precisely of that opinion," said the Scot; "and you will as soon convince me that a woman may be completely beautiful with fine eyes, good teeth, and a fair complexion, though she should not have a *nose* on her face, as that a landscape, or country, can be completely beautiful without a mountain." "Well, but here are mountains enough," resumed the other; "look around you." "Mountains!" cried the Caledonian, "very pretty mountains, truly! They call that Castel Gondolfo of theirs a castle too, and a palace, forsooth! but does that make it a residence fit for a Prince?" "Why, upon my word, I do not think it much amiss," said the other; "it looks full as well as the palace of St. James's." "The palace of St. James's," exclaimed the Scot, "is a scandal to the nation; it is both a shame and a sin, that so great a monarch as the King of Scotland, England, and Ireland, with his Royal consort, and their large family of small children, should live in a shabby old cloister, hardly good enough for monks. The palace of Holyrood-house, indeed, is a residence meet for a king." "And the gardens; pray what sort of gardens have you belonging to that palace?" said the Englishman; "I have been told you do not excel in those." "But we excel in gardeners," replied the other, "which are as much preferable as the creator is preferable to the created." "I am surprised, however," rejoined the South Briton, "that, in a country like yours, where there are so many creators, so very few fruit-gardens are created." "Why, Sir, it is not to be expected," said Mr. B——, "that anyone country will excel in every thing. Some enjoy a climate more favourable for peaches, and vines, and nectarines; but, by G—, Sir, no country on earth produces better men and women than Scotland." "I dare say none does," replied the other. "So as France excels in wines, England in wool and oxen, Arabia in horses, and other countries in other animals, you imagine Scotland excels all others in the human species." "What I said, Sir, was, that the human species in no country excel those in Scotland; and that I assert again, and will maintain, Sir, to my last gasp." "I do not intend to deny it," said the Englishman; "but you will permit me to observe, that, men being its staple commodity, it must be owned that Scotland carries on a brisk trade; for I know no country that has a greater *exportation*; you will find Scotchmen in all the countries of the world." "So much the better for all the countries of the world," said Mr. B——; "for every body knows that the Scotch cultivate and improve the arts and sciences wherever they go." "They certainly improve their own fortunes wherever they go," rejoined the other;—"like their gardeners, though they can create little or nothing at home, they often create very good fortunes in other countries; and this is one reason of our having the pleasure of so much of their company in London." "Whether it affords you pleasure or not, Sir, nothing can be more certain," replied the Scot in the most serious tone, "than that you may *improve* very much by their company and example. But there are various reasons," continued he, "for so many of my countrymen sojourning in London. That city is now, in some measure, the capital of Scotland as well as of England. The seat of government is there; the King of Scotland, as well as of England, resides there; the Scotch nobility and gentry have as good a right to be near the person of their Sovereign as the English; and you must allow, that, if some Scotchmen make fortunes in England, many of our best estates are also spent there. But you mean to say, that the Scotch, in general, are poor in comparison of the English. This we do not deny, and cannot possibly forget, your countrymen refresh our memories with it so often. We allow, therefore, that you have this advantage over us;—and the Persians had the same over the Macedonians at the battle of Arbela. But, whether Scotland be poor or rich, those Scots who settle in England must carry industry, talents, or wealth with them, otherwise they will starve there as well as elsewhere; and when one country draws citizens of this description from another, I leave you to judge which has the most reason to complain. And let me tell you, Sir, upon the whole, the advantages which England derives from the Union, are manifest and manifold." "I cannot say," replied the Englishman, "that I have thought much on this subject; but I shall be obliged to you if you will enumerate a few of them." "In the first place," resumed the Scot, "Has she not greatly increased in wealth since that time?" "She has so," replied the other, smiling, "and I never knew the *real cause* before." "In the next place, Has she not acquired a million and a half of subjects, who otherwise would have been with her enemies? For this, *and other reasons*, they are equivalent to three millions. In the third place, Has she not acquired security? without which riches are of no value. There is no door open *now*, Sir, by which the French can enter into your country. They dare as soon be d—— as attempt to invade Scotland; so if you can defend your own coast, there is no fear of you; but without a perfect union with Scotland, England could not enjoy the principal benefit she derives from her insular situation." "Not till Scotland should be subdued," said the Englishman. "Subdued!" repeated the astonished Scot; "let me tell you, Sir, *that* is a very strange hypothesis; the fruitless attempts of many centuries might have taught you that the thing is impossible; and, if you are conversant in history, you will find, that, after the decline of the Roman Empire, the course of conquest was from *the North to the South*." "You mean," said the South Briton, "that Scotland would have conquered England." "Sir," replied the other, "I think the English as brave a nation as ever existed, and therefore I will not say that the Scotch are braver; far less shall I assert, that *they*, consisting of only a fifth part of the numbers, could subdue the English; but I am sure, that rather than submit they would try; and you will admit that the trial would be no advantage to either country." "Although I am fully convinced," said the Englishman, "how the experiment would end, I should be sorry to see it made, particularly at this time." "Yet, Sir," rejoined the Scot, "there are people of your country, as I am told, who, even at *this time*, endeavour to exasperate the minds of the inhabitants of one part of Great Britain against the natives of the other, and to create dissension between two countries, whose mutual safety depends on their good agreement; two countries whom Nature herself, by separating them from the rest of the world, and encircling them with her azure bond of union, seems to have intended for one." "I do assure you, my good Sir," said the English Gentleman, "I am not of the number of those who wish to raise such dissension. I love the Scotch; I always thought them a sensible and gallant people; and some of the most valued friends I have on earth, are of your country." "You are a man of honour and discernment," said the Caledonian, seizing him eagerly by the hand; "and I protest, without prejudice or partiality, that I never knew a man of that character who was not of your way of thinking."

[7] The intervening words are cold, and not much connected with the fine line which concludes the quotation.

LETTER LXX.

We arrived in this city the third day after leaving Rome, though I have delayed writing till now. I wished to know something of the place, and to be a little acquainted with the people. The last is not difficult; because the Florentines are naturally affable, and the hospitality and politeness of the British Minister afford his countrymen frequent opportunities of forming an acquaintance with the best company in Florence. This gentleman has been here about thirty years, and is greatly esteemed by the Florentines. It is probably owing to this circumstance, and to the magnificent stile in which some English Noblemen live, who have long resided here, that the English, in general, are favourites with the inhabitants of this place. L——d C——r's conduct and disposition confirm them in the opinion they long have had of the good-nature and integrity of the nation to which he belongs. His Lady is of an amiable character, and affords them a very favourable specimen of English beauty.

We have had no opportunity of seeing the Grand Duchess. She is of a domestic turn, and lives much in the country with her children, of which she has a comfortable number; but the Grand Duke having come to town for two days, we had the honour of being presented to him at the Palazzo Pitti. There is a striking resemblance of each other in all the branches of the Austrian family. Wherever I had met with the Grand Duke, I should immediately have known that he belonged to it. He, as well his brother who resides at Milan, has, in a remarkable degree, the thick lip; which has long been a distinguishing feature in the Austrian family. He is a handsome man, is rapid in his words and motions, and has more vivacity in his manner than either the Emperor or Archduke; like them, he is good-humoured, condescending and affable. After the extinction of the Medici family, the Florentines grumbled on account of the disadvantage and inconveniency of having Sovereigns who did not reside among them. They exclaimed that their money was carried away to a distant country, and the most profitable offices at home filled by foreigners. They have now got a Sovereign who resides and spends his revenue among them, and has provided the State most plentifully in heirs; yet they still grumble. They complain of the taxes—But in what country of Europe is there not the same complaint?

Florence is, unquestionably, a very beautiful city. Independent of the churches and palaces, some of which are very magnificent, the architecture of the houses in general is in a good taste, the streets are remarkably clean, and paved with large broad stones, chiseled so as to prevent the horses from sliding. This city is divided into two unequal parts by the river Arno, over which there are no less than four bridges in sight of each other. That called the Ponte della Trinità, is uncommonly elegant. It is built entirely of white marble, and ornamented with four beautiful statues, representing the Four Seasons. The quays, the buildings on each side, and the bridges, render that part of Florence through which the river runs, by far the finest. The same is the case at Paris; and it happens fortunately for those two cities, that those parts are almost constantly before the eye, on account of the necessity people are continually under of passing and repassing those bridges; whereas in London, whose river and bridges are far superior to any in France or Italy, people may live whole seasons, attend all the public amusements, and drive every day from one end of the town to the other, without ever seeing the Thames or the bridges, unless they go on purpose. For this reason, when a foreigner is asked which he thinks the finest city, Paris or London; the moment Paris is mentioned, the Louvre, and that striking part which is situated between the Pont Royal and Pont Neuf, presents itself to his imagination. He can recollect no part of London equal in magnificence to this; and ten to one, if he decides directly, it will be in favour of Paris: but if he takes a little more time, and compares the two capitals, street by street, square by square, and bridge with bridge, he will probably be of a different opinion. The number of inhabitants in Florence is calculated by some at eighty thousand. The streets, squares, and fronts of the palaces are adorned with a great number of statues; some of them by the best modern masters, Michael Angelo, Bandinelli, Donatello, Giovanni di Bologna, Benvenuto, Cellini, and others. A taste for the arts must be kept alive, independent almost of any other encouragement, in a city where so many specimens are continually before the eyes of the inhabitants. There are towns in Europe, where statues, exposed night and day within the reach of the common people, would run a great risque of being disfigured and mutilated; here they are as safe as if they were shut up in the Great Duke's gallery.

Florence has been equally distinguished by a spirit for commerce and for the fine arts; two things which are not always united. Some of the Florentine merchants formerly were men of vast wealth, and lived in a most magnificent manner. One of them, about the middle of the fifteenth century, built that noble fabric, which, from the name of its founder, is still called the Palazzo Pitti. The man was ruined by the prodigious expence of this building, which was immediately purchased by the Medici family, and has continued, ever since, to be the residence of the Sovereigns. The gardens belonging to this palace are on the declivity of an eminence. On the summit there is a kind of fort, called Belvedere. From this, and from some of the higher walks, you have a complete view of the city of Florence, and the beauteous vale of Arno, in the middle of which it stands. The prospect is bounded on every side by an amphitheatre of fertile hills, adorned with country-houses and gardens. In no part of Italy, that I have seen, are there so many villas, belonging to private persons, as in the neighbourhood of this city; the habitations of the peasants, likewise, seem much more neat and commodious. The country all around is divided into small farms, with a neat farm-house on each. Tuscany produces a considerable quantity of corn, as well as excellent wine, and great quantities of silk. The peasants have a look of health and contentment: the natural beauty of the Italian countenance not being disgraced by dirt, or deformed by misery, the women in this country seem handsomer, and are, in reality, more blooming, than in other parts of Italy. When at work, or when they bring their goods to market, their hair is confined by a silk net, which is also much worn at Naples; but on holidays they dress in a very picturesque manner. They do not wear gowns, but a kind of jacket without sleeves. They have no other covering for the upper part of the arm but their shift sleeves, which are tied with riband. Their petticoats are generally of a scarlet colour. They wear ear-rings and necklaces. Their hair is adjusted in a becoming manner, and adorned with flowers. Above one ear they fix a little straw hat; and on the whole have a more gay, smart, coquetish air, than any country-girls I ever saw.

Churches, and palaces, and statues, are no doubt ornamental to a city; and the Princes are praise-worthy who have taken pains to rear and collect them; but the greatest of all ornaments are cheerful, happy, living countenances. The taste is not general; but, I thank God, I know some people who, to a perfect knowledge and unaffected love of the fine arts, join a passion for a collection of this kind, who cannot, without uneasiness, see one face in a different style, and whose lives and fortunes are employed in smoothing the corrosions of penury and misfortune, and *restoring* the *original* air of satisfaction and cheerfulness to the human countenance. Happy the people whose Sovereign is inspired with this species of virtù!

LETTER LXXI.

Florence.

I have generally, since our arrival at Florence, passed two hours every forenoon in the famous gallery. Connoisseurs, and those who wish to be thought such, remain much longer. But I plainly feel this is enough for me; and I do not think it worth while to prolong my visit after I begin to be tired, merely to be thought what I am not. Do not imagine, however, that I am blind to the beauties of this celebrated collection; by far the most valuable now in the world.

One of the most interesting parts of it, in the eyes of many, is the series of Roman Emperors, from Julius Cæsar to Gallienus, with a considerable number of their Empresses, arranged opposite to them. This series is almost complete; but wherever the bust of an Emperor is wanting, the place is filled up by that of some other distinguished Roman. Such an honour is bestowed with great propriety on Seneca, Cicero, or Agrippa, the son-in-law of Augustus. But, on perceiving a head of Antinous, the favourite of Adrian, among them, a gentleman whispered me,—*that* minion, pointing to the head, would not have been admitted into such company any where but in Florence. It ought, however, to be remembered, that the Gallery is not an Ægyptian court of judicature, where Princes are tried, after death, for crimes committed during their life. If the vices of originals had excluded their portraits, what would have become of the series of Roman Emperors, and particularly of the bust of the great Julius himself, who was husband to all the wives and — — —— —— The gallery is sacred to art, and every production which she avows, has a right to a place here.

Amidst those noble specimens of ancient sculpture, some of the works of Michael Angelo are not thought undeserving a place. His Bacchus and Faunus, of which the well-known story is told, have been by some preferred to the two antique figures representing the same.

The beautiful head of Alexander is universally admired by all the virtuosi; though they differ in opinion with regard to the circumstance in which the sculptor has intended to represent that hero. Some imagine he is dying; Mr. Addison imagines he sighs for new worlds to conquer; others that he faints with pain and loss of blood from the wounds he received at Oxydrace. Others think the features express not bodily pain or languor, but sorrow and remorse, for having murdered his faithful friend Clitus. You see how very uncertain a business this of a virtuoso is. I can hardly believe that the artist intended simply to represent him dying; there was nothing very creditable in the manner he brought on his death. Nor do I think he would choose to represent him moaning, or languishing with pain or sickness; there is nothing heroic in that; nor do we sympathise so readily with the pains of the body, as with those of the mind. As for the story of his weeping for new worlds, he will excite still less sympathy, if that is the cause of his affliction. The last conjecture, therefore, that the artist intended to represent him in a violent fit of remorse, is the most probable. The unfinished bust of Marcus Brutus, by Michael Angelo, admirably expresses the determined firmness of character which belonged to that virtuous Roman. The artist, while he wrought at this, seems to have had in his mind Horace's Ode

Justum et tenacem propositi virum

Non civium ardor prava jubentium,

Non vultus instantis tyranni

Mente quatit solidâ, &c.

This would, in my opinion, be a more suitable inscription for the bust, than the concetto of Cardinal Bembo, which is at present under it[8]. Michael Angelo, in all probability was pleased with the expression he had already given the features, and chose to leave it as an unfinished sketch, rather than risk weakening it by an attempt to improve it.

The virtuosi differ in opinion respecting the Arrotino, or Whetter, as much as about the head of Alexander. A young gentleman said to an antiquarian, while he contemplated the Arrotino, "I believe, Sir, it is imagined that this statue was intended for the slave, who, while he was whetting his knife, overheard Catiline's conspiracy."—"That is the vulgar opinion," said the other; "but the statue was, in reality, done for a peasant, who discovered the plot into which the two sons of Junius Brutus entered for the restoration of Tarquin." "I ask pardon, Sir," said the young man; "but although one may easily see that the figure listens with the most exquisite expression of attention, yet I should think it very difficult to delineate in the features, whether the listener heard a conspiracy, or any thing else which greatly interested him, and absolutely impossible to mark, by any expression of countenance, what particular conspiracy he is hearing." "Your observation is just, young man," said the antiquarian, "when applied to modern artists, but entirely the reverse when applied to the ancient. Now, for my own part, I plainly perceive in that man's countenance, and after you have studied those matters as profoundly as I have done you will see the same, that it is the conspiracy for the restoration of Tarquin, and no other plot whatever, which he listens to; as for Catiline's conspiracy, it is not possible he could know any thing about it; for, good God! people ought to reflect, that the man must have been dead four hundred years before Catiline was born."

As we are now in the famous octogonal room, called Tribuna, I ought, if I had any thing new to say, to descant a little on the distinguishing excellencies of the Dancing Faun, the Wrestlers, the Venus Urania, the Venus Victrix; and I would most willingly pay the poor tribute of my praise to that charming figure known by the name of Venus de Medicis. Yet, in the midst of all my admiration, I confess I do not think her equal to her brother Apollo in the Vatican. In that sublime figure, to the most perfect features and proportions, is joined an air which seems more than human. The Medicean Venus is unquestionably a perfect model of female beauty; but while Apollo appears more than a man, the Venus seems precisely a beautiful woman.

In the same room are many valuable curiosities, besides a collection of admirable pictures by the best masters. I do not know whether any are more excellent of their kind, but I am convinced none are more attentively considered than the two Venuses of Titian; one is said to be a portrait of his wife, the other of his mistress. The first is the fined portrait I ever saw, except the second; of this you have seen many copies: though none of them equals the beauty of the original, yet they will give a juster idea of it than any description of mine could. On the back ground, two women seem searching for something in a trunk. This episode is found much fault with; for my part, I see no great harm the two poor women do: none but those critics who search more eagerly after *deformity* than *beauty*, will take any notice of them.

Besides the Gallery and Tribuna, the hundredth part of whose treasures I have not particularised, there are other rooms, whose contents are indicated by the names they bear; as, the Cabinet of Arts, of Astronomy, of Natural History, of Medals, of Porcelain, of Antiquities, and the Saloon of the Hermaphrodite, so called from a statue which divides the admiration of the Amateurs with that in the Borghese village at Rome. The excellence of the execution is disgraced by the vileness of the subject. We are surprised how the Greeks and Romans could take pleasure in such unnatural figures; in this particular their taste seems to have been as depraved, as in general it was elegant and refined. In this room there is a collection of drawings by some of the greatest masters, Michael Angelo, Raphael, Andrea del Sarto, and others. There is, in particular, a sketch of the Last Judgment by the first-named of these painters, different, and, in the opinion of some, designed with more judgment, than his famous picture on the same subject in Sixtus the Fourth's chapel in the Vatican.

The large room, called the Gallery of Portraits, is not the least curious in this vast Musæum. It contains the portraits, all executed by themselves, of the most eminent painters who have flourished in Europe during the three last centuries. They amount to above two hundred; those of Rubens, Vandyke, Rembrandt, and Guido, were formerly the most esteemed; two have been added lately, which vie with the finest in this collection—those of Meng's and Sir Joshua Reynolds. The portrait of Raphael seems to have been done when he was young; it is not equal to any of the above. The Electress Dowager of Saxony has made a valuable addition to this collection, by sending her own portrait painted by herself; she is at full length, with the palette and pencils in her hands. Coreggio, after hearing the picture of St. Cecilia at Bologna cried up as a prodigy, and the *ne plus ultra* of art, went to see it; and conscious that there was nothing in it that required the exertion of greater powers than he felt within himself, he was overheard to say, "Anch' io sono pittore." This illustrious princess was also conscious of her powers when she painted this portrait, which seems to pronounce to the spectators, *Anch' io sono pittrice.*

[8]

Dum Bruti effigiem Michael de marmore fingit,

In mentem sceleris venit, et abstinuit.

LETTER LXXII.

Having now crossed from the Adriatic to the Mediterranean, and travelled through a considerable part of Italy, I acknowledge I have been agreeably disappointed in finding the state of the poorer part of the inhabitants less wretched than, from the accounts of some travellers, I imagined it was; and I may with equal truth add, that although I have not seen so much poverty as I was taught to expect, yet I have seen far more poverty than misery. Even the extremity of indigence is accompanied with less wretchedness here than in many other countries. This is partly owing to the mildness of the climate and fertility of the soil, and partly to the peaceable, religious, and contented disposition of the people. The miseries which the poorer part of mankind suffer from cold, are, perhaps, greater than those derived from any other source whatever. But in Italy, the gentleness of the climate protects them from this calamity nine months of the year. If they can gather as much wood as to keep a moderate fire during the remaining three, and procure a coarse cloke, they have little to fear from that quarter. Those who cannot get employment, which is often the case in this country, and even those who do not choose to work, which is the case with numbers all the world over, receive a regular maintenance from some convent: with this, and what little they can pick up otherwise, in a country where provisions are plentiful and cheap, they pass through life, in their own opinion, with more satisfaction than if they had a greater number of conveniencies procured by much bodily labour. Whereas in Great Britain, Germany, and other northern countries, the poor have no choice but to work; for if they remain idle, they are exposed to miseries more intolerable than the hardest labour can occasion to the laziest of mankind; they are invaded at once by the accumulated agonies of hunger and cold; and if they have ever had sufficient credit to contract a little debt, they are continually in danger of being thrown into a jail among pickpockets and felons. With respect to the lowest of the tradespeople and the day-labourers in this country, their wages are certainly not high; nor are they willing, by great efforts of industry, to gain all they might; but what they do gain is never wasted in intemperance, but fairly spent in their families on the real necessaries and comforts of life.

The Italians are the greatest loungers in the world, and while walking in the fields, or stretched in the shade, seem to enjoy the serenity and genial warmth of their climate with a degree of luxurious indulgence peculiar to themselves. Without ever running into the daring excesses of the English, or displaying the frisky vivacity of the French, or the invincible phlegm of the Germans, the Italian populace discover a species of sedate sensibility to every source of enjoyment, from which, perhaps, they derive a greater degree of happiness than any of the other. The frequent processions and religious ceremonies, besides amusing and comforting them, serve to fill up their time, and prevent that ennui and those immoral practices which are apt to accompany poverty and idleness. It is necessary, for the quiet and happiness of every community, that the populace be employed. Some politicians imagine, that their whole time should be spent in gainful industry. Others think, that though the riches of the state will not be augmented, yet the general happiness, which is a more important object, will be promoted by blending the occupations of industry with a considerable proportion of such superstitious ceremonies as awaken the future hopes, without lulling the present benevolence, of the multitude; but nobody can doubt, that in countries where, from whatever cause, industry does not prevail, processions and other rites of the same nature will tend to restrain the populace from the vices, and of consequence prevent some of the miseries of idleness.

The peasantry of this country are unquestionably in a more comfortless state than a benevolent mind could wish them. But, England and Switzerland excepted, is not this the case all over Europe? In all the countries I have seen, or had an account of, the husbandmen, probably the most virtuous, but certainly the most useful part of the community, whose labour and industry maintain all the rest, and in whom the real strength of the state resides, are, by a most unjust dispensation, generally the poorest and most oppressed. But although the Italian peasantry are by no means in the affluent, independent situation of the peasantry of Switzerland, and the tenantry of England, yet they are not subjected to the same oppressions with those of Germany, nor are they so poor as those of France.

Great part of the lands in Italy belong to convents; and I have observed, and have been assured by those who have the best opportunities of knowing, that the tenants of these communities are happier, and live more at their ease, than those of a great part of the nobility. The revenues of convents are usually well managed, and never allowed to be squandered away by the folly or extravagance of any of its members; consequently the community is not driven, by craving and threatening creditors, as individuals frequently are, to squeeze out of their vassals the means of supplying the waste occasioned by their own vanity and expence. A convent can have no incitement to severe and oppressive exactions from the peasants, except sheer avarice; a passion which never rises to such a height in a society where the revenue is in common, as in the breast of an individual, who is solely to reap the fruits of his own oppression.

The stories which circulate in Protestant countries, concerning the scandalous debauchery of monks, and the luxurious manner in which they live in their convents, whatever truth there may have been in them formerly, are certainly now in a great measure without foundation. I remember when

I was at the Grande Chartreuse, near Grenoble, which has a considerable district of land belonging to it, I was informed, and this information was confirmed by what I saw, that those monks were gentle and generous masters, and that their tenants were envied by all the peasantry around, on account of the treatment they received, and the comparatively easy terms on which they held their farms. From the enquiries I have made in France, Germany, and Italy, I am convinced that this is usually the case with those peasants who belong to convent lands; and very often, I have been informed, besides having easy rents, they also find affectionate friends and protectors in their masters, who visit them in sickness, comfort them in all distresses, and are of service to their families in various shapes.

I have been speaking hitherto of the peasantry belonging to convents; but I believe I might extend the remark to the tenants of ecclesiastics in general, though they are often represented as more proud and oppressive masters than any class of men whatever; an aspersion which may have gained credit the more easily on this account, that instances of cruelty and oppression in ecclesiastics strike more, and raise a greater indignation, than the same degree of wickedness in other men; they raise a greater indignation, because they are more unbecoming of clergymen, and they strike more when they do happen, because they happen seldomer. The ambition of Popes some centuries ago, when the Court of Rome was in its zenith, the unlimited influence and power which particular Churchmen acquired in England and France, had those effects upon their actions and characters, which ambition and power usually have on the characters of men; it rendered them insolent, unfeeling, and persecuting. Yet, for every cruel and tyrannical Pope that history has recorded, it will be easy to name two or three Roman Emperors who have surpassed them in every species of wickedness; and England and France have had Prime Ministers with all the vices, without the abilities, of Wolsey and Richelieu.

Those who declaim against the wickedness of the clergy, seem to take it for granted that this body of men were the authors of the most horrid instances of persecution, massacre, and tyranny, over men's consciences, that are recorded in the annals of mankind; yet Philip II., Charles IX. and Henry VIII. were not Churchmen; and the capricious tyranny of Henry, the frantic fury of Charles, and the persevering cruelty of Philip, seem to have proceeded from the personal characters of these Monarchs, or to have been excited by what they considered as their political interest, rather than by the suggestions of their Clergy.

As the subjects of the Ecclesiastical State are perhaps the poorest in Italy, this has been imputed to the rapacious disposition which some assert is natural to Churchmen. This poverty, however, may be otherwise accounted for. Bishop Burnet very judiciously observes, that the subjects of a government, which is at once despotic and elective, labour under peculiar disadvantages; for an hereditary Prince will naturally have considerations for his people which an elective one will not, "unless he has a degree of generosity not common among men, and least of all among Italians, who have a passion for their families which is not known in other places[9]." An elective Prince, knowing that it is only during his reign that his family can receive any benefit from it, makes all the haste he can to enrich them. To this it may be added, that as Popes generally arrive at Sovereignty at an age when avarice predominates in the human breast, they may be supposed to have a stronger bias than other Princes to that sordid passion; and even when this does not take place, their needy relations are continually prompting them to acts of oppression, and suggesting ways and means of squeezing the people. Other causes might be assigned; but, that it does not originate from the imputation above mentioned, seems evident from this, that the peasants of particular ecclesiastics, and of the convents in the Pope's dominions, as well as in other countries, are generally less oppressed than those of the lay lords and princes.

From what has been thrown out by some celebrated wits, and the common-place invective of those who affect that character, one would be led to imagine that there is something in the nature of the clerical profession which has a tendency to render men proud and oppressive. Such indiscriminating censure carries no conviction to my mind, because it is contradicted by the experience I have had in life, and by the observations, such as they are, which I have been able to make on human nature. I do not mean, in imitation of the satirists above mentioned, to put the Clergy of all religions on the same footing. My opportunities of knowledge are too slender to justify *that*; my acquaintance with this order of men having been in a great measure confined to those of the Protestant Church, men of learning and ingenuity, of quiet, speculative, and benevolent dispositions; it is usually, indeed, this turn of mind which has inclined them to the ecclesiastical profession. But though my acquaintance with the Roman Catholic Clergy is very limited, yet the few I do know could not be mentioned as exceptions to what I have just said of the Protestant; and, exclusive of all personal knowledge of the men, it is natural to think that the habitual performance of the ceremonies of the Christian religion, though intermingled with some superstitious rites, and the preaching the doctrines of benevolence and good-will towards men, must have some influence on the lives and characters of those who are thus employed. It is a common error, prevailing in Protestant countries, to imagine that the Roman Catholic Clergy laugh at the religion they inculcate, and regard their flocks as the dupes of an artful plan of imposition. By far the greater part of Roman Catholic priests and monks are themselves most sincere believers, and teach the doctrines of Christianity, and all the miracles of the legend, with a perfect conviction of their divinity and truth. The few who were behind the curtain when falsehood was first embroidered upon truth, and those who have at different periods been the authors of all the masks and interludes which have enriched the grand drama of superstition, have always chosen to employ such men, being sensible that the inferior actors would perform their parts more perfectly, by acting from nature and real conviction. "Paulum interesse censes," says Davus to Mysis, "ex animo omnia ut fert natura, facias an de industria[10]."

The accounts we receive of their gluttony, are often as ill-founded as those of their infidelity. The real character of the majority of monks and inferior ecclesiastics, both in France and Italy, is that of a simple, superstitious, well-meaning race of men, who for the most part live in a very abstemious and mortified manner, notwithstanding what we have heard of their gluttony, their luxury, and voluptuousness. Such accusations are frequently thrown out by those who are ill entitled to make them. I remember being in company with an acquaintance of yours, who is distinguished for the delicacy of his table and the length of his repasts, from which he seldom retires without a bottle of Burgundy for his own share, not to mention two or three glasses of Champaign between the courses. We had dined a few miles from the town in which we then lived, and were returning in his chariot; it was winter, and he was wrapped in fur to the nose. As we drove along, we met two friars walking through the snow; little threads of icicles hung from their beards; their legs and the upper part of their feet were bare, but their soles were defended from the snow by wooden sandals. "There goes a couple of dainty rogues," cried your friend as we drew near them; "only think of the folly of permitting such lazy, luxurious rascals to live in a State, and eat up the portion of the poor. I will engage that those two scoundrels, as lean and mortified as they look, will devour more victuals in a day, than would maintain two industrious families." He continued railing against the luxury of those two friars, and afterwards expatiated upon the epicurism of the clergy in general; who, he said, were all alike in every country, and of every religion. When we arrived in town, he told me he had ordered a little nice supper to be got ready at his house by the time of our return, and had lately got some excellent wine, inviting me at the same time to go home with him; for, continued he, as *we have driven* three miles in such weather, *we stand in great need* of some refreshment.

That in all Roman Catholic countries, and particularly in Italy, the clergy are too numerous, have too much power, too great a proportion of the lands, and that some of them live in great pomp and luxury, is undeniable. That the common people would be in a better situation, if manufactures and the spirit of industry could be introduced among them, is equally true; but, even as things are, I cannot help thinking that the state of the Italian peasantry is preferable, in many respects, to that of the peasants of many other countries in Europe. They are not beaten by their ecclesiastical lords, as those of Germany are by their masters, on every real or imaginary offence. They have not their children torn from them, to be sacrificed to the pomp, avarice, or ambition of some military despot; nor are they themselves pressed into the service as soldiers for life.

In England and in France the people take an interest in all national disputes, and consider the cause of their country or their Prince as their own; they enter into the service voluntarily, and fight with ardour for the glory of the country or King they love. Those ideas enable them to submit to a thousand hardships without repining, and they feel the sensations of happiness in the midst of toil, want, and danger. But in Germany, where the passions are annihilated, and a man is modelled into a machine before he is thought a good soldier, where his blood is sold by the Prince to the highest bidder, where he has no quarrel with the enemy he murders, and no allegiance to the Monarch for whom he fights, the being liable to be forced into such a service, is one of the most dreadful of all calamities. Yet a regiment of such compelled soldiers, dressed in gaudy uniform, and powdered for a review, with music sounding and colours flying, makes a far more brilliant appearance than a cluster of peasants with their wives and children upon a holiday. But if we could examine the breasts of the individuals, we should find in those of the former nothing but the terror of punishment, hatred of their officers, distrust of each other, and life itself supported only by the hope of desertion; while the bosoms of the latter are filled with all the affections of humanity, undisturbed by fear or remorse.

[9] Vide Bishop Burnet's Travels.

[10] Andria Terentii.

LETTER LXXIII.

Society seems to be on an easy and agreeable footing in this city. Besides the conversazionis which they have here, as in other towns of Italy, a number of the nobility meet every day at a house called the Casino. This society is pretty much on the same footing with the clubs in London. The members are elected by ballot. They meet at no particular hour, but go at any time that is convenient. They play at billiards, cards, and other games, or continue conversing the whole evening, as they think proper. They are served with tea, coffee, lemonade, ices, or what other refreshments they choose; and each person pays for what he calls for. There is one material difference between this and the English clubs, that women as well as men are members.

The company of both sexes behave with more frankness and familiarity to strangers, as well as to each other, than is customary in public assemblies in other parts of Italy.

The Opera at Florence is a place where the people of quality pay and receive visits, and converse as freely as at the Casino above mentioned. This occasions a continual passing and repassing to and from the boxes, except in those where there is a party of cards formed; it is then looked on as a piece of ill manners to disturb the players. I never was more surprised, than when it was proposed to me to make one of a whist party, in a box which seemed to have been made for the purpose, with a little table in the middle. I hinted that it would be full as convenient to have the party somewhere else; but I was told, good music added greatly to the pleasure of a whist party; that it increased the joy of good fortune, and soothed the affliction of bad. As I thought the people of this country better acquainted than myself with the power of music, I contested the point no longer; but have generally played two or three rubbers at whist in the stage-box every opera night.

From this you may guess, that, in this city, as in some other towns in Italy, little attention is paid to the music by the company in the boxes, except at a new opera, or during some favourite air. But the dancers command a general attention: as soon as they begin, conversation ceases; even the card-players lay down their cards, and fix their eyes on the Ballette. Yet the excellence of Italian dancing seems to consist in feats of strength, and a kind of jerking agility, more than in graceful movement. There is a continual contest among the performers, who shall spring highest. You see here none of the sprightly, alluring gaiety of the French comic dancers, nor of the graceful attitudes, and smooth flowing motions of the performers in the serious opera at Paris. It is surprising, that a people of such taste and sensibility as the Italians, should prefer a parcel of athletic jumpers to elegant dancers.

On the evenings on which there is no opera, it is usual for the genteel company to drive to a public walk immediately without the city, where they remain till it begins to grow duskish. Soon after our arrival at Florence, in one of the avenues of this walk we observed two men and two ladies, followed by four servants in livery. One of the men wore the insignia of the garter. We were told this was the Count Albany, and that the Lady next to him was the Countess. We yielded the walk, and pulled off our hats. The gentleman along with them was the Envoy from the King of Prussia to the Court of Turin. He whispered the Count, who, returning the salutation, looked very earnestly at the D—— of H——. We have seen them almost every evening since, either at the opera or on the public walk. His G—does not affect to shun the avenue in which they happen to be; and as often as we pass near them, the Count fixes his eyes in a most expressive manner upon the D——, as if he meant to say—our ancestors were better acquainted.

You know, I suppose, that the Count Albany is the unfortunate Charles Stuart, who left Rome some time since on the death of his father, because the Pope did not think proper to acknowledge him by the title which he claimed on that event. He now lives at Florence, on a small revenue allowed him by his brother. The Countess is a beautiful woman, much beloved by those who know her, who universally describe her as lively, intelligent, and agreeable. Educated as I was in Revolution principles, and in a part of Scotland where the religion of the Stuart family, and the maxims by which they governed, are more reprobated than perhaps in any part of Great Britain, I could not behold this unfortunate person without the warmest emotion and sympathy. What must a man's feelings be, who finds himself excluded from the most brilliant situation, and noblest inheritance that this world affords, and reduced to an humiliating dependance on those, who, in the natural course of events, should have looked up to him for protection and support? What must his feelings be, when on a retrospective view he beholds a series of calamities attending his family, that is without example in the annals of the unfortunate; calamities, of which those they experienced after their accession to the throne of England, were only a continuation? Their misfortunes began with their royalty, adhered to them through ages, increased with the increase of their dominions, did not forsake them when dominion was no more; and, as he has reason to dread, from his own experience, are not yet terminated. It will afford no alleviation or comfort, to recollect that part of this black list of calamities arose from the imprudence of his ancestors; and that many gallant men, in England, Scotland, and Ireland, have at different periods been involved in their ruin.

Our sympathy for this unfortunate person is not checked by any blame which can be thrown on himself. He surely had no share in the errors of the first Charles, the profligacy of the second, or the impolitic and bigotted attempts of James against the laws and established religion of Great Britain and Ireland; therefore, whilst I contemplate with approbation and gratitude the conduct of those patriots who resisted and expelled that infatuated monarch, ascertained the rights of the subject, and settled the constitution of Great Britain on the firm basis of freedom on which it has stood ever since the Revolution, and on which I hope it will ever stand, yet I freely acknowledge, that I never could see the unfortunate Count Albany without sentiments of compassion, and the most lively sympathy.

I write with the more warmth, as I have heard of some of our countrymen, who, during their tours through Italy, made the humble state to which he is reduced a frequent theme of ridicule, and who, as often as they met him in public, affected to pass by with an air of sneering insult. The motive to this is as base and abject as the behaviour is unmanly; those who endeavour to make misfortune an object of ridicule, are themselves the objects of detestation. A British nobleman or gentleman has certainly no occasion to form an intimacy with the Count Albany; but while he appears under that name, and claims no other title, it is ungenerous, on every accidental meeting, not to behave to him with the respect due to a man of high rank, and the delicacy due to a man highly unfortunate.

One thing is certain; that the same disposition which makes men insolent to the weak, renders them slaves to the powerful; and those who are most apt to treat this unfortunate person with an ostentatious contempt at Florence, would have been his most abject flatterers at St. James's.

LETTER LXXIV.

In a country where men are permitted to speak and write without restraint on the measures of government; where almost every citizen may flatter himself with the hopes of becoming a part of the legislature; where eloquence, popular talents, and political intrigues, lead to honours, and open a broad road to wealth and power; men, after the first glow of youth is past, are more obedient to the loud voice of ambition than to the whispers of love. But in despotic states, and in monarchies which verge towards despotism, where the will of the prince is law; or, which amounts nearly to the same thing, where the law yields to the will of the prince; where it is dangerous to speak or write on general politics, and death or imprisonment to censure the particular measures of government; love becomes a first, instead of being a secondary object; for ambition is, generally speaking, a more powerful passion than love; and on this account women are the objects of greater attention and respect in despotic than in free countries. That species of address to women which is now called gallantry, was, if I am not mistaken, unknown to the ancient Greeks and Romans; nothing like it appears in any of Terence's comedies, where one would naturally expert to find it, if any such thing had existed when they were written. It now prevails, in some degree, in every country of Europe, but appears in different forms according to the different characters, customs, and manners, of the various countries.

In the courts of Germany it is a formal piece of business; etiquette governs the arrows of Cupid, as well as the torch of Hymen. Mistresses are chosen from the number of quarters on their family coats of arms, as well as from the number of their personal charms; and those ladies who are well provided in the first, seldom are without lovers, however deficient they may be in the second. But though many avenues, which in England lead to power and distinction, are shut up in Germany, and the whole power of government is vested in the sovereign, yet the young nobility cannot bestow a great deal of their time in gallantry. The military profession, which in the time of peace is perfect idleness in France and England, is a very serious, unremitting employment in Germany. Men who are continually drilling soldiers, and whose fortunes and reputations depend on the expertness of the troops under their command, cannot pay a great deal of attention to the ladies.

Every French gentleman must be a soldier; but fighting is the only part of the business they go through with spirit; they cannot submit to the German precision in discipline, their souls sink under the tediousness of a campaign, and they languish for a battle from the impetuosity of their disposition, and impatience to have the matter decided one way or the other. This, with many particular exceptions, is the general style of the French noblesse; they all serve an apprenticeship to war, but gallantry is the profession they follow for life. In England, the spirit of play and of party draws the minds of the young men of fortune from love or gallantry; those who spend their evenings at a gaming house, or in parliament, seldom think of any kind of women but such as may be had without trouble; and, of course, women of character are less attended to than in some other countries. When I was last at Paris, the Marquis de F—— found an English newspaper on my table; it contained a long and particular account of a debate which had happened in both houses of parliament; he read it with great attention while I finished a letter, and then throwing down the paper, he said to me, "Mais, mon ami, pendant que vos messieurs s'amusent a jaser comme cela dans votre chambre des pairs et votre parlement[11], parbleu un etranger auroit beau jeu avec leurs femmes."

Intrigues of gallantry, comparatively speaking, occur seldom in England; and when they do, they generally proceed from a violent passion, to which every consideration of fortune and reputation is sacrificed, and the business concludes in a flight to the continent, or a divorce.

They manage matters otherwise in France; you hardly ever hear of flights or divorces in that country; a hundred new arrangements are made, and as many old ones broken, in a week at Paris, without noise or scandal; all is conducted quietly et felon les régles; the fair sex are the universal objects of respect and adoration, and yet there is no such thing as constancy in the nation. Wit, beauty, and every accomplishment united in one woman, could not fix the volatility of a Frenchman; the love of variety, and the vanity of new conquests, would make him abandon this phœnix for birds far less rare and estimable. The women in France, who are full of spirit and sensibility, could never endure such usage, if they were not as fickle and as fond of new conquests as their lovers.

In Italy, such levity is viewed with contempt, and constancy is, by both sexes, still classed among the virtues.

That high veneration for the fair sex which prevailed in the ages of chivalry, continued long after in the form of a sentimental platonic kind of gallantry. Every man of ingenuity chose unto himself a mistress, and directly proclaimed her beauty and her cruelty in love ditties, madrigals, and elegies, without expecting any other recompence than the reputation of a constant lover and a good poet. By the mere force of imagination, and the eloquence of their own metaphysical sonnets, they became persuaded that their mistresses were possessed of every accomplishment of face and mind, and that themselves were dying for love.

As in those days women were constantly guarded by their fathers and brothers before marriage, and watched and confined by their husbands for the rest of their lives; the refined passions above described were not exposed to the same accidents which so frequently befal those of modern lovers; they could neither fall into a decay from a more perfect knowledge of the ladies character, nor were they liable to sudden death from enjoyment. But whilst the women were adored in song, they were miserable in reality; confinement and distrust made them detest their husbands, and they endeavoured to form connections with men more to their taste than either jealous husbands or metaphysical lovers. To treat a woman of character as if she were an unprincipled wanton, is the most likely way to make her one. In those days of jealousy, a continual trial of skill seems to have subsisted between husband and wife, as if every lord, soon after marriage, had told his lady, "Now, Madam, I know perfectly well what you would be at; but it is my business to prevent you: I'll guard you so well, and watch you so closely, that it shall never be in your power to gratify your inclinations." "You are perfectly in the right, my lord," replied the lady, with all meekness, "pray guard and watch as your wisdom shall direct; I, also, shall be vigilant on my part, and we shall see how the business will end." The business generally did end as might have been expected; and the only consolation left the husband was, to endeavour to assassinate the happy lover.

But when French manners began to spread over Europe, and to insinuate themselves among nations the most opposite in character to the French, jealousy was first held up as the most detestable of all the passions. The law had long declared against its dismal effects, and awful denunciations had been pronounced from the pulpit against those who were inflamed by its bloody spirit; but without effect, till ridicule joined in the argument, and exposed those husbands to the contempt and derision of every fashionable society, who harboured the gloomy dæmon in their bosoms.

As in England, after the Restoration, people, to shew their aversion to the Puritans, turned every appearance of religion into ridicule, and from the extreme of hypocrisy flew at once to that of profligacy; so in Italy, from the custom of secluding the wife from all mankind but her husband, it became the fashion that she should never be seen with her husband, and yet always have a man at her elbow.

I shall conclude what I have to say on this subject in my next.

[11] The French in general are apt to make the same mistake with the Marquis; they often speak of the House of Peers and the *Parliament* as two distinct assemblies.

LETTER LXXV.

Florence.

Before the Italian husbands could adopt or reconcile their minds to a custom so opposite to their former practice, they took some measures to secure a point which they had always thought of the highest importance. Finding that confinement was a plan generally reprobated, and that any appearance of jealousy subjected the husband to ridicule, they agreed that their wives should go into company and attend public places, but always attended by a friend whom they could trust, and who, at the same time, should not be disagreeable to the wife. This compromise could not fail of being acceptable to the women, who plainly perceived that they must be gainers by any alteration of the former system; and it soon became universal all over Italy, for the women to appear at public places leaning upon the arm of a man; who, from their frequently whispering together, was called her Cicisbeo. It was stipulated, at the same time, that the lady, while abroad under his care, should converse with no other man but in his presence, and with his approbation; he was to be her guardian, her friend, and gentleman-usher.

The custom at present is, that this obsequious gentleman visits the lady every forenoon at the toilet, where the plan for passing the evening is agreed upon; he disappears before dinner, for it is usual all over Italy for the husband and wife to dine together tête-à-tête, except on great occasions, as when there is a public feast. After dinner the husband retires, and the Cicisbeo returns and conducts the lady to the public walk, the conversazioné, or the opera; he hands her about wherever she goes, presents her coffee, sorts her cards, and attends with the most pointed assiduity till the amusements of the evening are over; he accompanies her home, and delivers up his charge to the husband, who is then supposed to resume his functions.

From the nature of this connection, it could not be an easy matter to find a Cicisbeo who would be equally agreeable to the husband and wife. At the beginning of the institution, the husbands, as I have been informed, preferred the platonic swains, who professed only the metaphysicks of love, and whose lectures, they imagined, might refine their wives ideas, and bring them to the same way of thinking; in many instances, no doubt, it would happen, that the platonic admirer asked with *less seraphic ends*; but these instances serve only as proofs that the husbands were mistaken in their men; for however absurd it may appear in the eyes of some people, to imagine that the husbands believe it is only a platonic connection which subsists between their wives and the Cicisbeos; it is still more absurd to believe, as some strangers who have passed through this country seem to have done, that this whole system of Cicisbeism was from the beginning, and is now, an universal system of adultery connived at by every Italian husband. To get clear of one difficulty, those gentlemen fall into another much more inexplicable; by supposing that the men, who of all the inhabitants of Europe were the most scrupulous with regard to their wives chastity, should acquiesce in, and in a manner become subservient to, their prostitution. In support of this strange doctrine, they assert, that the husbands being the Cicisbeos of other women, cannot enjoy this privilege on any other terms; and are therefore contented to sacrifice their wives for the sake of their mistresses. That some individuals may be profligate enough to act in this manner, I make no doubt. Similar arrangements we hear instances of in every country; but that such a system is general, or any thing near it, in Italy, seems to me perfectly incredible, and is contrary to the best information I have received since I have been here. It is also urged, that most of the married men of quality in Italy act in the character of Cicisbeo to some woman or other; and those who are not Platonic lovers, ought to suspect that the same liberties are taken with their wives which they take with the spouses of their neighbours; and therefore their suffering a man to visit their wives in the character of a cavaliero servente, is in effect conniving at their own cuckoldom. But this does not follow as an absolute consequence; for men have a wonderful faculty of deceiving themselves on such occasions. So great is the infatuation of their vanity, that the same degree of complaisance, which they consider as the effect of a very natural and excusable weakness, when indulged by any woman for themselves, they would look on as a horrible enormity if admitted by their wives for another man; so that whatever degree of licentiousness may exist in consequence of this system, I am convinced the majority of husbands make exceptions in their own favour, and that their ladies find means to satisfy each individual that he is not involved in a calamity, which, after all, is more general in other countries, as well as Italy, than it ought.

Even when there is the greatest harmony and love between the husband and wife, and although each would prefer the other's company to any other, still, such is the tyranny of fashion, they must separate every evening; he to play the cavaliero servente to another woman, and she to be led about by another man. Notwithstanding this inconveniency, the couples who are in this predicament are certainly happier than those whose affections are not centered at home. Some very loving couples lament the cruelty of this separation, yet the world in general seem to be of opinion, that a man and his wife who dine together every day, and lie together every night, may, with a proper exertion of philosophy, be able to support being asunder a few hours in the evening.

The Cicisbeo, in many instances, is a poor relation or humble friend, who, not being in circumstances to support an equipage, is happy to be admitted into all the societies, and to be carried about to public diversions, as an appendage to the lady. I have known numbers of those gentlemen, whose appearance and bodily infirmities carried the clearest refutation, with respect to themselves personally, of the scandalous stories of an improper connection between cavaliero serventes and their mistresses. I never in my life saw men more happily formed, both in body and mind, for saving the reputation of the females with whom they were on a footing of intimacy. The humble and timid air which many of them betray in the presence of the ladies, and the perseverance with which they continue their services, notwithstanding the contemptuous stile in which they are often treated, is equally unlike the haughtiness natural to favoured lovers, and the indifference of men satiated with enjoyment.

There are, it must be confessed, Cicisbeos of a very different stamp, whose figure and manners might be supposed more agreeable to the ladies they serve, than to their lords. I once expressed my surprise, that a particular person permitted one of this description to attend his wife. I was told, by way of solution of my difficulty, that the husband was poor, and the Cicisbeo rich. It is not in Italy only where infamous compromises of this nature take place.

I have also known instances, since I have been in this country, where the characters of the ladies were so well established, as not to be shaken either in the opinion of their acquaintances or husbands, although their cavaliero serventes were in every respect agreeable and accomplished.

But whether the connection between them is supposed innocent or criminal, most Englishmen will be astonished how men can pass so much of their time with women. This, however, will appear less surprising, when they recollect that the Italian nobility dare not intermeddle in politics; can find no employment in the army or navy; and that there are no such amusements in the country as hunting or drinking. In such a situation, if a man of fortune has no turn for gaming, what can he do? Even an Englishman, in those desperate circumstances, might be driven to the company and conversation of women, to lighten the burden of time. The Italians have persevered so long in this expedient, that, however extraordinary it may seem to those who have never tried it, there can be no doubt that they find it to succeed. They tell you, that nothing so effectually sooths the cares, and beguiles the tediousness of life, as the company of an agreeable woman; that though the intimacy should never exceed the limits of friendship, there is something more flattering and agreeable in it than in male friendships; that they find the female heart more sincere, less interested, and warmer in its attachments; that women in general have more delicacy, and——. Well, well, all this may be true, you will say; but may not a man enjoy all these advantages, to as great perfection, by an intimacy and friendship with his own wife, as with his neighbour's? "Non, Monsieur, point du tout," answered a Frenchman, to whom this question was once addressed. "Et pourquoi donc? Parceque cela n'est pas permis." This you will not think a very satisfactory answer to so natural and so pertinent a question—It is not the fashion! This, however, was the only answer I received all over Italy.

This system is unknown to the middle and lower ranks; they pass their time in the exercise of their professions, and in the society of their wives and children, as in other countries; and in that sphere of life, jealousy, which formed so strong a feature of the Italian character, is still to be found as strong as ever. He who attempts to visit the wife or mistress of any of the tradespeople without their permission, is in no small danger of a Coltellata. I have often heard it asserted, that Italian women have remarkable powers of attaching their lovers. Those powers, whatever they are, do not seem to depend entirely on personal charms, as many of them retain their ancient influence over their lovers after their beauty is much in the wane, and they themselves are considerably advanced in the vale of years. I know an Italian nobleman, of great fortune, who has been lately married to a very beautiful young woman, and yet he continues his assiduity to his former mistress, now an old woman, as punctually as ever. I know an Englishman who is said to be in the same situation, with this difference, that his lady is still more beautiful. In both these instances, it is natural to believe that the beautiful young wives will always take care to keep their husbands in such a chaste and virtuous way of thinking, that, whatever time they may spend with their ancient mistresses, nothing criminal will ever pass between them.

Whatever satisfaction the Italians find in this kind of constancy, and in their friendly attachments to one woman, my friend the Marquis de F—— told me, when I last saw him at Paris, that he had tried it while he remained at Rome, and found it quite intolerable. A certain obliging ecclesiastic had taken the trouble, at the earnest request of a lady of that city, to arrange matters between her and the Marquis, who was put into immediate possession of all the rights that were ever supposed to belong to a Cicisbeo. The woman nauseated her husband, which had advanced matters mightily; and her passion for the Marquis was in proportion to her abhorrence of the other. In this state things had remained but a very short time, when the Marquis called one afternoon to drive the Abbé out a little into the country, but he happened to have just dined. The meals or this ecclesiastic were generally rather oppressive for two or three hours after they were finished; he therefore declined the invitation, saying, by way of apology, "Je suis dans les horreurs de la digestion." He then enquired how the Marquis's amour went on with the lady. "Ah, pour l'amour, cela est à peu près passé," replied the Marquis, "et nous sommes actuellement dans les horreurs de l'amitié."

LETTER LXXVI.

The Florentines imputed the decay of the republic to the circumstance of their Sovereign residing in another country; and they imagined, that wealth would accumulate all over Tuscany, and flow into Florence, from various quarters, as soon as they should have a residing Prince, and a Court established. It appears, that their hopes were too sanguine, or at least premature. Commerce is still in a languid condition, in spite of all the pains taken by the Great Duke to revive it.

The Jews are not held in that degree of odium, or subjected to the same humiliating distinctions here, as in most other cities of Europe. I am told, some of the richest merchants are of that religion. Another class of mankind, who are also reprobated in some countries, are in this looked on in the same light with other citizens. I mean the actors and singers at the different Theatres. Why Christians, in any country, should have the same prejudice against them as against Jews, many are at a loss to know; it cannot, certainly, be on the same account. Actors and actresses have never been accused of an obstinate, or superstitious adherence to the principles or ceremonies of any *false religion* whatever.

To attempt a description of the churches, palaces, and other public buildings, would lead, in my opinion, to a very unentertaining detail. Few cities, of its size, in Europe, however, afford so fine a field of amusement to those who are fond of such subjects; though the lovers of architecture will be shocked to find several of the finest churches without fronts, which, according to some, is owing to a real deficiency of money; while others assert, they are left in this condition, as a pretext for levying contributions to finish them.

The chapel of St. Lorenzo is, perhaps, the finest and most expensive habitation that ever was reared for the dead; it is encrusted with precious stones, and adorned by the workmanship of the best modern sculptors. Some complain that, after all, it has a gloomy appearance. There seems to be no impropriety in that, considering what the building was intended for; though, certainly, the same effect might have been produced at less expence. Mr. Addison remarked, that this chapel advanced so very slowly, that it is not impossible but the family of Medicis may be extinct before their burial-place is finished. This has actually taken place: the Medici family is extinct, and the chapel remains still unfinished.

Of all the methods by which the vanity of the Great has distinguished them from the rest of mankind, this of erecting splendid receptacles for their bones, excites the least envy. The sight of the most superb edifice of this kind, never drew a repining sigh from the bosom of one poor person; nor do the unsuccessful complain, that the bodies of Fortune's favourites rot under Parian marble, while their own will, in all probability, be allowed to moulder beneath a plain turf.

I have already mentioned the number of statues which ornament the streets and squares of Florence, and how much they are respected by the common people. I am told, they amount in all to above one hundred and fifty, many of them of exquisite workmanship, and admired by those of the best taste. Such a number of statues, without any drapery, continually exposed to the public eye, with the far greater number of pictures, as well as statues, in the same state, to be seen in the palaces, have produced, in both sexes, the most perfect insensibility to nudities.

Ladies who have remained some time at Rome and Florence, particularly those who affect a taste for virtù, acquire an intrepidity and a cool minuteness, in examining and criticising naked figures, which is unknown to those who have never passed the Alps. There is something in the figure of the God of Gardens, which is apt to alarm the modesty of a novice; but I have heard of female dilettantes who minded it no more than a straw.

The Palazzo Pitti, where the Great Duke resides, is on the opposite side of the Arno from the Gallery. It has been enlarged since it was purchased from the ruined family of Pitti. The furniture of this palace is rich and curious, particularly some tables of Florentine work, which are much admired. The most precious ornaments, however, are the paintings. The walls of what is called the Imperial Chamber, are painted in fresco, by various painters; the subjects are allegorical, and in honour of Lorenzo of Medicis, distinguished by the name of the Magnificent. There is more fancy than taste displayed in those paintings. The other principal rooms are distinguished by the names of Heathen Deities, as Jupiter, Apollo, Mars, Venus, and by paintings in fresco, mostly by Pietro da Cortona. In the last mentioned, the subjects are different from what is naturally expected from the name of the room, being representations of the triumphs of Virtue over Love, or some memorable instance of continency. As the Medici family have been more distinguished for the protection they afforded the arts, than for the virtues of continency or self-denial, it is probable, the subject, as well as the execution of these pieces, was left entirely to the painter.

I happened lately to be at this palace, with a person who is perfectly well acquainted with all the pictures of any merit in Florence. While he explained the peculiar excellencies of Pietro's manner, a gentleman in company, who, although he does not pretend to the smallest skill in pictures, would rather remain ignorant for ever, than listen to the lectures of a connoisseur, walked on, by himself, into the other apartments, while I endeavoured to profit by my instructor's knowledge. When the other gentleman returned, he said, "I know no more of painting than my pointer; but there is a picture in one of the other rooms, which I would rather have than all those you seem to admire so much; it is the portrait of a healthy, handsome, country woman, with her child in her arms. There is nothing interesting in the subject, to be sure, because none of us are personally acquainted with the woman. But I cannot help thinking the colours very natural. The young woman's countenance is agreeable, and expressive of fondness and the joy of a mother over a first-born. The child is a robust, chubby-cheeked fellow; such as the son of a peasant should be."

We followed him into the room, and the picture which pleased him so much, was the famous Madonna della Seggiola of Raphael. Our instructor immediately called out Viva! and pronounced him a man of genuine taste; because, without any previous knowledge or instruction, he had fixed his admiration on the finest picture in Florence. But this gentleman, as soon as he understood what the picture was, disclaimed all title to praise; "because," said he, "although, when I considered that picture, simply as the representation of a blooming country wench hugging her child, I admired the art of the painter, and thought it one of the truest copies of nature I ever saw; yet, I confess, my admiration is much abated, now that you inform me his intention was to represent the Virgin Mary." "Why so?" replied the Cicerone; "the Virgin Mary was not of higher rank. She was but a poor woman, living in a little village in Galilee." "No rank in life," said the other, "could give additional dignity to the person who had been told by an Angel from heaven, that she had found favour with God; that her Son should be called the Son of the Highest; and who, herself, was conscious of all the miraculous circumstances attending his conception and birth. In the countenance of such a woman, besides comeliness, and the usual affection of a mother, I looked for the most lively expression of admiration, gratitude, virgin modesty, and divine love. And when I am told, the picture is by the greatest painter that ever lived, I am disappointed in perceiving no traces of that kind in it." What justice there is in this gentleman's remarks, I leave it to better judges than I pretend to be, to determine.

After our diurnal visit to the Gallery, we often pass the rest of the forenoon in the gardens belonging to this palace. The vale of Arno; the gay hills that surround it; and other natural beauties to be viewed from thence, form an agreeable variety, even to eyes which have been feasting on the most exquisite beauties of art. The pleasure arising from both, however, diminishes by repetition; but may be again excited by the admiration of a new spectator, of whose taste and sensibility you have a good opinion. I experienced this on the arrival of Mr. F——r, a gentleman of sense, honour, and politeness, whose company gave fresh relish to our other enjoyments in this place. It is now some time since he left us; and I am not at all unhappy in the thoughts of proceeding, in a day or two, to Bologna, in our road to Milan.

LETTER LXXVII.

Milan.

For a post or two after leaving Florence, and about as much before you arrive at Bologna, the road is very agreeable; the rest of your journey between those two cities is over the sandy Apennines.

We had the good fortune to find at Bologna Sir William and Lady H——, Mr. F——t, Mr. K——, Lord L——, and Sir H—— F——n. Our original intention was to have proceeded without delay to Milan, but on such an agreeable meeting it was impossible not to remain a few days at Bologna.

I went to the academy on the day of distributing the prizes for the best specimens and designs in painting, sculpture, and architecture; a discourse in praise of the fine arts was pronounced by one of the professors, who took that opportunity of enumerating the fine qualities of the Cardinal Legate; none of the virtues, great or small, were omitted on the occasion; all were attributed in the superlative degree to this accomplished prince of the church. The learned orator acknowledged, however, that this panegyric did not properly belong to his subject, but hoped that the audience, and particularly the Legate himself, who was present, would forgive him, in consideration that the eulogy had been wrung from him by the irresistible force of truth. The same force drew forth something similar in praise of the Gonfalonier and other magistrates who were present also; and what you may think very remarkable, the number and importance of the qualities attributed to those distinguished persons kept an exact proportion with their *rank*. Power in this happy city seems to have been weighed in the scales of justice, and distributed by the hand of wisdom. All the inferior magistrates, we were informed, are very worthy men, endowed with many excellent qualities; the Gonfalonier has many more, and the Legate possesses every virtue under the sun. If the Pope had entered the room, the too lavish professor would not have been able to help him to a single morsel of praise which had not been already served up.

This town is at present quite full of strangers, who came to assist at the procession of Corpus Domini. The Duke of Parma, several Cardinals, and other persons of high distinction, besides a prodigious crowd of citizens, attended this great festival. The streets through which the Host was carried under a magnificent canopy, were adorned with tapestry, paintings, looking-glasses, and all the various kinds of finery which the inhabitants could produce. Many of the paintings seemed unsuitable to the occasion; they were on profane, and some of them on wanton subjects; and it appeared extraordinary to see the figures of Venus, Minerva, Apollo, Jupiter, and others of that abdicated family, arranged along the walls in honour of a triumph of the Corpus Christi.

On our way to Milan we stopped a short time at Modena, the capital of the duchy of that name. The whole duchy is about fifty miles in length, and twenty-six in breadth; the town contains twenty thousand inhabitants; the streets are in general large, straight, and ornamented with porticoes. This city is surrounded by a fortification, and farther secured by a citadel; it was anciently rendered famous by the siege which Decimus Brutus sustained here against Marc Antony.

We proceeded next to Parma, a beautiful town, considerably larger than Modena, and defended, like it, by a citadel and regular fortification. The streets are well built, broad, and regular. The town is divided unequally by the little river Parma, which loses itself in the Po, ten or twelve miles from this city.

The theatre is the largest of any in Europe; and consequently a great deal larger than there is any occasion for. Every body has observed, that it is so favourable to the voice, that a whisper from the stage is heard all over this immense house; but nobody tells us on what circumstance in the construction this surprising effect depends.

The Modenese was the native country of Correggio, but he passed most of his life at Parma. Several of the churches are ornamented by the pencil of that great artist, particularly the cupola of the cathedral; the painting of which has been so greatly admired for the grandeur of the design and the boldness of the fore-shortenings. It is now spoiled in such a manner, that its principal beauties are not easily distinguished.

Some of the best pictures in the Ducal Palace have been removed to Naples and elsewhere; but the famous picture of the Virgin, in which Mary Magdalen and St. Jerom are introduced, still remains. In this composition, Correggio has been thought to have united, in a supreme degree, beauties which are seldom found in the same piece; an excellence in any one of which has been sufficient to raise other artists to celebrity. The same connoisseurs assert, that this picture is equally worthy of admiration, on account of the freshness of the colouring, the inexpressible gracefulness of the design, and the exquisite tenderness of the expression. After I had heard all those fine things said over and over again, I thought I had nothing to do but admire; and I had prepared my mind accordingly.—Would to Heaven that the respectable body of connoisseurs were agreed in opinion, and I should most readily submit mine to theirs! But while the above eulogium still resounded in my ears, other connoisseurs have asserted, that this picture is full of affectation; that the shadowing is of a dirty brown, the attitude of the Magdalen constrained and unnatural; that she may strive to the end of time without ever being able to kiss the foot of the infant Jesus in her present position; that she has the look of an ideot; and that the Virgin herself is but a vulgar figure, and seems not a great deal wiser; that the angels have a ridiculous simper, and most abominable air of affectation; and finally, that St. Jerom has the appearance of a sturdy beggar, who intrudes his brawny figure where it has no right to be.

Distracted with such opposite sentiments, what can a plain man do, who has no great reliance on his own judgment, and wishes to give offence to neither party? I shall leave the picture as I found it, to answer for itself, with a single remark in favour of the angels. I cannot take upon me to say how the real angels of heaven look; but I certainly have seen some *earthly* angels, of my acquaintance, assume the simper and air of those in this picture, when they wished to appear quite celestial.

The duchies of Modena, Parma, and Placentia, are exceedingly fertile. The soil is naturally rich, and the climate being moister here than in many other parts of Italy, produces more plentiful pasturage for cattle. The road runs over a continued plain, among meadows and corn fields, divided by rows of trees, from whose branches the vines hang in beautiful festoons. We had the pleasure of thinking, as we drove along, that the peasants are not deprived of the blessings of the smiling fertility among which they live. They had in general a neat, contented, and cheerful appearance. The women are successfully attentive to the ornaments of dress, which is never the case amidst oppressive poverty.

Notwithstanding the fertility of the country around it, the town of Placentia itself is but thinly inhabited, and seems to be in a state of decay. What first strike a stranger on entering this city, are two equestrian statues, in bronze, by Giovanni di Bologna; they stand in the principal square, before the Town-house. The best of the two represents that consummate general Alexander Farnese, Duke of Parma and Placentia, who commanded the army of Philip II. in the Netherlands. The inscription on the pedestal mentions his having relieved the city of Paris, when called to the assistance of the League into France, where his great military skill, and cool intrepidity, enabled him to baffle all the ardent impetuosity of the gallant Henry. He was certainly worthy of a better master, and of serving in a better cause. We cannot, without regret, behold a Prince, of the Duke of Parma's talents and character, supporting the pride of an unrelenting tyrant, and the rancour of furious fanatics.

Except the Ducal Palace, and some pictures in the churches, which I dare swear you will cordially forgive me for passing over undescribed, I believe there is not a great deal in this city worthy of attention; at all events I can say little about them, as we remained here only a few hours during the heat of the day, and set out the same evening for Milan.

LETTER LXXVIII.

Milan.

Milan, the ancient capital of Lombardy, is the largest city in Italy, except Rome; but though it is thought rather to exceed Naples in size, it does not contain above one-half the number of inhabitants.

The cathedral stands in the centre of the city, and, after St. Peter's, is the most considerable building in Italy. It ought by this time to be the largest in the world, if what they tell us be true, that it is near four hundred years since it was begun, and that there has been a considerable number of men daily employed in completing it ever since; but as the injuries which time does to the ancient parts of the fabric keep them in constant employment, without the possibility of their work being ever completed, Martial's epigram, on the barber Eutrapelus, has been applied to them with great propriety. That poor man, it seems, performed his operations so very slowly, that the beards of his patients required shaving again on the side where he had begun, by the time he had finished the other.

EUTRAPELUS TONSOR DUM CIRCUIT ORA LUPERCI,
EXPUNGITQUE GENAS, ALTERA BARBA SUBIT.

No church in Christendom is so much loaded, I had almost said disfigured, with ornaments. The number of statues, withinside and without, is prodigious; they are all of marble, and many of them finely wrought. The greater part cannot be distinctly seen from below, and therefore certainly have nothing to do above. Besides those which are of a size, and in a situation to be distinguished from the street, there are great numbers of smaller statues, like fairies peeping from every cornice, and hid among the grotesque ornaments, which are here in vast profusion. They must have cost much labour to the artists who formed them, and are still a source of toil to strangers, who, in compliment to the person who harangues on the beauties of this church, which he says is the eighth wonder of the world, are obliged to ascend to the roof to have a nearer view of them.

This vast fabric is not simply encrusted, which is not uncommon in Italy, but intirely built of solid white marble, and supported by fifty columns, said to be eighty-four feet high. The four pillars under the cupola, are twenty-eight feet in circumference. By much the finest statue belonging to it is that of St. Bartholomew. He appears flayed, with his skin flung around his middle like a sash, and in the easiest and most degagé manner imaginable. The muscles are well expressed; and the figure might be placed with great propriety in the hall of an anatomist; but, exposed as it is to the view of people of all professions, and of both sexes, it excites more disgust and horror than admiration. Like those beggars who uncover their sores in the street, the artist has destroyed the very effect he meant to produce. This would have sufficiently evinced that the statue was not the work of Praxitiles, without the inscription on the pedestal.

NON ME PRAXITILES, SED MARCUS FINXIT AGRATI.

The inside of the choir is ornamented by some highly esteemed sculpture in wood. From the roof hangs a case of crystal, surrounded by rays of gilt metal, and inclosing a nail, said to be one of those by which our Saviour was nailed to the cross. The treasury belonging to this church is reckoned the richest in Italy, after that of Loretto. It is composed of jewels, relics, and curiosities of various kinds; but what is esteemed above all the rest, is a small portion of Aaron's rod, which is carefully preserved there.

The Ambrosian Library is said to be one of the most valuable collections of books and manuscripts in Europe. It is open a certain number of hours every day; and there are accommodations for those who come to read or make extracts.

In the Museum, adjoining to the Library, are a considerable number of pictures, and many natural curiosities. Among these they shew a human skeleton. This does not excite a great deal of attention, till you are informed that it consists of the bones of a Milanese Lady, of distinguished beauty, who, by her last will, ordained that her body should be dissected, and the skeleton placed in this Museum, for the contemplation of posterity. If this Lady only meant to give a proof of the transient nature of external charms, and that a beautiful woman is not more desirable after death than a homely one, she might have allowed her body to be consigned to dust in the usual way. In spite of all the cosmetics, and other auxiliaries which vanity employs to varnish and support decaying beauty and flaccid charms, the world have been long satisfied that death is not necessary to put the fair and the homely on a level; a very few years, even during life, do the business.

There is no place in Italy, perhaps I might have said in Europe, where strangers are received in such an easy, hospitable manner, as at Milan. Formerly the Milanese Nobility displayed a degree of splendour and magnificence, not only in their entertainments, but in their usual style of living, unknown in any other country in Europe. They are under a necessity at present of living at less expence, but they still shew the same obliging and hospitable disposition. This country having, not very long since, been possessed by the French, from whom it devolved to the Spaniards, and from them to the Germans, the troops of those nations have, at different periods, had their residence here, and, in the course of these vicissitudes, produced a style of manners, and stamped a character on the inhabitants of this duchy, different from what prevails in any other part of Italy; and nice observers imagine they perceive in Milanese manners the politeness, formality, and honesty imputed to those three nations, blended with the ingenuity natural to Italians. Whatever uneasiness the inhabitants of Milan may feel, from the idea of their being under German government, they seem universally pleased with the personal character of Count Fermian, who has resided here many years as Minister from Vienna, equally to the satisfaction of the Empress Queen, the inhabitants of Milan, and the strangers who occasionally travel this way.

The Great Theatre having been burnt to the ground last year, there are no dramatic entertainments, except at a small temporary playhouse, which is little frequented; but the company assemble every evening in their carriages on the ramparts, and drive about, in the same manner as at Naples, till it is pretty late. In Italy, the ladies have no notion of quitting their carriages at the public walks, and using their own legs, as in England and France. On seeing the number of servants, and the splendour of the equipages which appear every evening at the Corso on the ramparts, one would not suspect that degree of depopulation, and diminution of wealth, which we are assured has taken place within these few years all over the Milanese; and which, according to my information, proceeds from the burthensome nature of some late taxes, and the insolent and oppressive manner in which they are gathered.

The natural productions of this fertile country must occasion a considerable commerce, by the exportation of grain, particularly rice; cattle, cheese, and by the various manufactures of silken and velvet stuffs, stockings, handkerchiefs, ribands, gold and silver laces and embroideries, woollen and linen cloths, as well as by some large manufactures of glass, and earthen ware in imitation of china, which are established here. But I am told monopolies are too much protected here, and that prejudices against the profession of a merchant still exist in the minds of the only people who have money. These cannot fail to check industry, and depress the soul of commerce; and perhaps there is little probability that the inhabitants of Milan will overcome this unfortunate turn of mind while they remain under German dominion, and adopt German ideas. The peasants, though more at their ease than in many other places, yet are not so much so as might be expected in so very fertile a country. Why are the inhabitants of the rich plains of Lombardy, where Nature pours forth her gifts in such profusion, less opulent than those of the mountains of Switzerland? Because Freedom, whose influence is more benign than sunshine and zephyrs, who covers the rugged rock with soil, drains the sickly swamp, and clothes the brown heath in verdure; who dresses the labourer's face with smiles, and makes him behold his increasing family with delight and exultation; Freedom has abandoned the fertile fields of Lombardy, and dwells among the mountains of Switzerland.

LETTER LXXIX.

Chamberry.

We made so short a stay at Turin that I did not think of writing from thence. I shall now give you a sketch of our progress since my last.

We left Milan at midnight, and arrived the next evening at Turin before the shutting of the gates. All the approaches to that city are magnificent. It is situated at the bottom of the Alps, in a fine plain watered by the Po. Most of the streets are well built, uniform, clean, straight, and terminating on some agreeable object. The Strada di Po, leading to the palace, the finest and largest in the city, is adorned with porticoes equally beautiful and convenient. The four gates are also highly ornamental. There can be no more agreeable walk than that around the ramparts. The fortifications are regular and in good repair, and the citadel is reckoned one of the strongest in Europe. The royal palace and the gardens are admired by some. The apartments display neatness, rather than magnificence. The rooms are small, but numerous. The furniture is rich and elegant; even the floors attract attention, and must peculiarly strike strangers who come from Rome and Bologna; they are curiously inlaid with various kinds of wood, and kept always in a state of shining brightness. The pictures, statues, and antiquities in the palace are of great value; of the former there are some by the greatest masters, but those of the Flemish school predominate.

No royal family in Europe are more rigid observers of the laws of etiquette, than that of Sardinia; all their movements are uniform and invariable. The hour of rising, of going to mass, of taking the air; every thing is regulated like clock-work. Those illustrious persons must have a vast fund of natural good-humour, to enable them to persevere in such a wearisome routine, and support their spirits under such a continued weight of oppressive formality.

We had the satisfaction of seeing them all at mass; but as the D—— of H—— grows more impatient to get to England the nearer we approach it, he declined being presented at court, and we left Turin two days after our arrival.

We stopped a few hours, during the heat of the day, at a small village, called St. Ambrose, two or three posts from Turin. I never experienced more intense heat than during this day, while we were tantalized with a view of the snow on the top of the Alps, which seem to overhang this place, though, in reality, they are some leagues distant. While we remained at St. Ambrose there was a grand procession. All the men, women, and children, who were able to crawl, attended; several old women carried crucifixes, others pictures of the saint, or flags fixed to the ends of long poles; they seemed to have some difficulty in wielding them, yet the good old women tottered along as happy as so many young ensigns the first time they bend under the regimental colours. Four men, carrying a box upon their shoulders, walked before the rest. I asked what the box contained, and was informed by a sagacious looking old man, that it contained the bones of St. John. I enquired if all the Saint's bones were there; he assured me, that not even a joint of his little finger was wanting; "Because," continued I, "I have seen a considerable number of bones in different parts of Italy, which are said to be the bones of St. John." He smiled at my simplicity, and said the world was full of imposition; but nothing could be more certain, than that those in the box were the true bones of the Saint; he had remembered them ever since he was a child—and his father, when on his death-bed, had told him, on the *word of a dying man*, That they belonged to St. John and no other body.

At Novalezza, a village at the bottom of Mount Cenis, our carriages were taken to pieces, and delivered to Muleteers to be carried to Lanebourg. I had bargained with the Vitturino, before we left Turin, for our passage over the mountain in the chairs commonly used on such occasions. The fellow had informed us there was no possibility of going in any other manner; but when we came to this place, I saw no difficulty in being carried up by mules, which we all preferred, to the great satisfaction of our knavish conductor, who thereby saved the expence of one half the chairmen, for whose labour he was already paid.

We rode up this mountain, which has been described in such formidable terms, with great ease. At the top there is a fine verdant plain of five or six miles in length, we halted at an Inn, called Santa Croce, where Piedmont ends and Savoy begins. Here we were regaled with fried trout, catched in a large lake within sight, from which the river Doria arises, which runs to Turin in conjunction with the Po. Though we ascend no higher than this plain, which is the summit of Mount Cenis, the mountains around are much higher; in passing the plain we felt the air so keen, that we were glad to have recourse to our great-coats; which, at the bottom of the hill, we had considered as a very superfluous part of our baggage. I had a great deal of conversation in passing the mountain with a poor boy, who accompanied us from Novalezza to take back the mules; he told me he could neither read nor write, and had never been farther than Suza on one side of the mountain, and Lanebourg on the other. He spoke four languages, Piedmontese, which is his native language; this is a kind of Patois very different from Italian; the Patois of the peasants of Savoy, which is equally different from French; he also spoke Italian and French wonderfully well; the second he had learnt from the Savoyard chairmen, and the two last from Italian and French travellers whom he has accompanied over Mount Cenis, where he has passed his life hitherto, and which he seems to have no desire of leaving. If you chance to be consulted by any parent who inclines to send their sons abroad merely that they may be removed from London, and acquire modern languages in the most œconomical manner, you now know what place to recommend. In none where opportunities for this branch of education are equal, is living cheaper than at Mount Cenis, and I know nothing in which it has any resemblance to London, except that it stands on much the same quantity of ground. I asked this boy, why he did not learn English.—He had all the inclination in the world.—"Why don't you learn it then as well as French?" "On attrape le François, Monsieur, bon gré, mal gré," answered he, "mais Messieurs les Anglois parlent peu."

When we arrived at the North side of the mountain we dismissed our mules, and had recourse to our Alpian chairs and chairmen. The chairs are constructed in the simplest manner, and perfectly answer the purpose for which they are intended. The chairmen are strong-made, nervous, little fellows. One of them was betrothed to a girl at Lanebourg, and was to be married that evening. I could not, in conscience, permit him to have any part in carrying me, but directly appointed him to Jack's chair. The young fellow presented us all with ribbons, which we wore in our hats in honour of the bride. "Are you very fond of your mistress, friend," said I? "Il faut que je l'aime beaucoup," answered he, "puisque, pauvre garçon comme me voila, je donne trente livres au prêtre pour nous marier." To tax matrimony, and oblige the people who *beget and maintain* children to pay to those who *maintain* none, seems bad policy; and it is surprising that a prince who attends so minutely, as his Sardinian Majesty, to the welfare of his subjects, does not remedy so great an abuse.

As our carriers jogged zig-zag, according to the course of the road, down the mountain, they laughed and sung all the way. "How comes it," said I to the D———, "that chairmen are generally merrier than those they carry? To hear these fellows without seeing them, one would imagine that *we* had the laborious part, while *they* sat at their ease." "True," answered he; "and the same person might conclude, on hearing the bridegroom sing so cheerfully, that we were just going to be married and not he." We arrived in a short time at the Inn at Lanebourg, nothing having surprised me so much in the passage of this mountain, the difficulty and danger of which has been greatly exaggerated by travellers, as the facility with which we achieved it.

As soon as the scattered members of our carriages were joined together, we proceeded on our journey. The road is never level, but a continued ascent and descent along the side of high mountains. We sometimes saw villages situated at a vast height above us; at other times they were seen with difficulty in the vales, at an immense depth below us. The village of Modane stands in a hollow, surrounded by stupendous mountains. It began to grow dark when we descended from a great height into this hollow; we could only perceive the rugged summits, and sides of the mountains which encircle the village, but not the village itself, or any part of the plain at the bottom; we therefore seemed descending from the surface, by a dark abyss leading to the centre of the globe. We arrived safe at Modane, however, for the road is good in every respect, steepness excepted. Next morning we continued our course, by a miserable place called La Chambre, to Aiguebelle, a village of much the same description. According to some authors, this was the road by which Hannibal led his army into Italy. They assert, that the plain at the summit of Mount Cenis was the place where he rested his army for four days, and from which he showed his soldiers the fertile plains of Italy, and encouraged them to persevere: others assert that he led his army into Italy by Mount St. Bernard. This is a discussion into which I am not qualified to enter; but M———r G———l M———l, a gentleman of learning, probity, and great professional merit, in his way to Italy, where he now is, endeavoured to trace the route of the Carthaginian army with great attention; and imagines he has been successful in his researches. He has also ascertained the spots on which some of the most memorable battles were fought, by carefully comparing the description of Polybius, and other authors, with the fields of battle, and has detected many mistakes, which have prevailed on this curious subject; every where supporting his own hypothesis by arguments which none but one who has carefully perused the various authors, and examined the ground with a soldier's eye, could adduce. The same gentleman has likewise made some observations relating to the arms of the ancient Romans, and their tactics in general, which are equally new and ingenious, and which, it is hoped, he will in due time give to the public.

We arrived at the inn at Aiguebelle just in time to avoid an excessive storm of thunder and rain, which lasted with great violence through the whole night. Those who have never heard thunder in a very mountainous country, can form no idea of the loudness, repetition, and length of the peals we heard this night. Many of the inhabitants of those mountains have never seen better houses than their own huts, or any other country than the Alps. What a rugged, boisterous piece of work must they take this world to be!

I fancy you have by this time had enough of mountains and vallies, so if you please we shall skip over Montmelian to Chamberry, where we arrived the same day on which we left Aiguebelle. To-morrow we shall sleep at Geneva. I did not expect much sleep this night from the thoughts of it, and therefore have sat up almost till day-break writing this letter.

LETTER LXXX.

The D—— of H—— went some weeks ago to visit an acquaintance in one of the provinces of France. As I inclined rather to pass that time at Geneva, we agreed to meet at Paris, whither Jack and I are thus far on our way.

I must now fairly confess that I found myself so happy with my kind friends the Genevois, that I could not spare an hour from their company to write to you or any correspondent, unless on indispensable business. I might also plead, that you yourself have been in some measure the cause of my being seduced from my pen. In your last letter; which I found waiting for me at the post-house at Geneva, you mention a late publication in terms that gave me a curiosity to see it; and an English gentleman, who had the only copy which has as yet reached that city, was so obliging as to lend it me. The hours which I usually allot to sleep, were all I had in my power to pass alone; and they were very considerably abridged by this admirable performance. The extensive reading there displayed, the perspicuity with which historical facts are related, the new light in which many of them are placed, the depth of the reflections, and the dignity and nervous force of the language, all announce the hand of a master. If the author lives to complete his arduous undertaking, he will do more to dissipate the historical darkness which overshadows the middle ages, give a clearer *History of the Decline and Fall of the Roman Empire*, and fill up, in a more satisfactory manner, the long interval between ancient and modern history, than all the writers who have preceded him. This accounts for my long silence. You see I resume my pen the very first opportunity, after the causes I have assigned for it are removed, which ought to give the more weight to my apology.

As I have frequently been at Lyons, I chose, on this occasion, to return to Paris by Franche Comté and Champagne. We accordingly set out very early yesterday morning, and were by no means in high spirits when we left Geneva, and passed along the side of the lake, through the Pais de Vaud. The beauties of that country, though they astonish at first sight, yet, like the characters of the inhabitants, they improve on intimacy. Every time I have looked at the lake of Geneva, and its delightful environs, I have discovered something new to admire. As I entered the Canton of Bern, I often turned about, and at last withdrew my eyes from those favourite objects, with an emotion similar to what you feel on taking leave of a friend, whom you have reason to think you shall never see again.

The first place we came to, on entering France from the Canton of Bern, is a poor little town on an hill; I forget its name. While the postillion stopped to put something to rights about the harness, I stepped into a shop where they sold wooden shoes; and in the course of my conversation with a peasant, who had just purchased a pair for himself, and another for his wife, he said, "les Bernois sont bien à leur aise, Monsieur, pendant que nous autres François vivons tres durement, et cependant les Bernois sont des hérétiques." "Voilà," said an old woman, who sat in a corner reading her breviary; "voilà," said she, taking off her spectacles, and laying her beads on the book, "ce que je trouve incompréhensible."

This was, however, at the extremity of France, and in a province lately acquired; for it must be confessed, that it is not common for the French to imagine that any country whatever has the advantage of theirs in any one circumstance; and they certainly are not so apt to grumble as some of their neighbours, who have less reason. When I was last at Geneva, a French hair-dresser—Let me intreat you not to shew this to your friend ——, who is so fond of people of quality, that he thinks there is no *life* out of their company. He would pshaw, and curse my poor peasants, and old women, and hair-dressers, and accuse me of being too fond of such low company.

As for the old women, I am much mistaken if there are not at least as many to be found of both sexes in high life as in low; for the others, I declare I have no particular affection, but I am fond of strokes of nature and character, and must look for them where they are to be found. I introduce the present hair-dresser to your acquaintance, because, if I am not mistaken, he spoke the sentiments of his whole nation, high and low. You shall judge. This young fellow attended me every morning while I remained at Geneva; he had been a year or two at London; and while he dressed my hair, his tongue generally moved as quick as his fingers. He was full of his remarks upon London, and the fine people whose hair he pretended to have dressed. "Do you not think," said I, "that people may live very happily in that country?" "Mais—pour cela oui, Monsieur." "Do you think, then, they *are* happy?" "Pour cela, non, Monsieur." "Can you guess at the reason why they are not, though they have so much reason to be so?" "Oui, Monsieur, elle est toute simple." "Pray what is the reason they are not happy?" "C'est, qu'ils ne font pas destinés à l'être."

A very genteel young man, a Genevois, happened to call on me, for two minutes, while this friseur was with me. The young gentleman had passed some time at Paris, and was dressed exactly in the Parisian taste. "He has much the air of one of your countrymen," said I to the Frenchman, as soon as the other had left the room.

"Mon Dieu! quelle différence," cried the friseur. "For my part, I can see none," said I. "Monsieur," resumed he, "soyez persuadé qu'aucun Genevois ne sera jamais pris pour un François." "There are certainly some *petit-maîtres* to be found in this town," said I. "Pardonnez moi," replied he, "ils ne sont que petit-maîtres manqués."

"Did you ever see an Englishman," said I, "who might pass for a Frenchman?" "Jamais de la vie, Monsieur!" replied he, with an accent of astonishment.

"Suppose him," said I, "a man of quality?" "N'importe."

"But," continued I, "suppose he had lived several years at Paris, that he was naturally very handsome, and well made, that he had been educated by the best French dancing-master, his clothes made by the best French taylor, and his hair dressed by the most eminent friseur in Paris?" "C'est beaucoup, Monsieur, mais ce n'est pas assez."

"What!" exclaimed I, "would you still know him to be an Englishman?" "Assurément, Monsieur."

"What! before he spoke?" "Au premier coup d'œil, Monsieur."

"The Devil you would; but how?" "C'est que Messieurs les Anglois ont un air—une manière de se présenter—un—que sais-je moi—vous m'entendez bien, Monsieur—un certain air si Gau—"

"Quel air maraud?" "Enfin un air qui est charmant, si vous voulez, Monsieur," said he rapidly, "mais que le Diable m'emporte si c'est l'air François."

To-morrow I shall take a view of this town, and proceed immediately after breakfast to Paris: mean while I wish you very heartily good night.

LETTER LXXXI.

I Made a longer stay at Besançon than I intended, and am now about to inform you what detained me. The morning after the date of my last, as I returned to the inn from the parade, where I had been to see the troops, I met a servant of the Marquis de F——, who ran up to me the moment he knew me, and, in a breath, told me, that his master was at Besançon; that he had been exceedingly ill, and thought, by the physicians, in great danger; but his complaint having terminated in an ague, they had now the strongest hopes of his recovery. I desired to be conducted immediately to him.

I found the Marquis alone; pale, languid, and greatly emaciated. He expressed, however, equal pleasure and surprise at this unexpected visit; said, he had been in danger of making a very long journey, and added, with a smile, that no man had ever set out with less inclination, for he hated travelling alone, and this was the only journey he could ever take, without wishing some of his friends to accompany him. He rejoiced, therefore, that he had been recalled in time to meet me before I should pass on to Paris. "But tell me," continued he, "for I have ten thousand questions to ask—but let us take things in order; Eh bien, donnez nous donc des nouvélles du Pape? On nous a dit que vous aviez passé par la ceremonie de la Pantoufle. Ne pourroit on pas pendre au tragique une misère comme cela chez vous où le Saint Pere passe pour une *Babylonienne* de mauvaise vie?" Before I could make any answer I chanced to turn my eyes upon a person whom I had not before observed, who sat very gravely upon a chair in a corner of the room, with a large periwig in full dress upon his head.

The Marquis, seeing my surprise at the sight of this unknown person, after a very hearty fit of laughter, begged pardon for not having introduced me sooner to that gentleman (who was no other than a large monkey), and then told me, he had the honour of being attended by a physician, who had the reputation of possessing the greatest skill, and who *certainly* wore the largest periwigs of any doctor in the province. That one morning, while he was writing a prescription at his bed-side, this same monkey had catched hold of his periwig by one of the knots, and instantly made the best of his way out at the window to the roof of a neighbouring house, from which post he could not be dislodged, till the Doctor, having lost patience, had sent home for another wig, and never after could be prevailed on to accept of this, which had been so much disgraced. That, *enfin*, his valet, to whom the monkey belonged, had, ever since that adventure, obliged the culprit, by way of punishment, to sit quietly for an hour every morning, with the periwig on his head.—Et pendant ces moments de tranquilité je suis honoré de la société du vénérable personage. Then addressing himself to the monkey, "Adieu, mon ami, pour aujourdhui—au plaisir de vous revoir;" and the servant immediately carried Monsieur le Medecin out of the room.

Afraid that the Marquis might be the worse for talking so much, I attempted to withdraw, promising to return in the evening; but this I could not get him to comply with. He assured me, that nothing did him so much harm as holding his tongue; and that the most excessive headach he had ever had in his life, was owing to his having been two hours without speaking, when he made his addresses to Madam de ———; who could never forgive those who broke in upon the thread of her discourse, and whom he *lost* after all, by uttering a few sentences before she could recover her breath after a fit of sneezing. In most people's discourse, added he, a sneeze passes for a full stop. "Mais dans le Caquet eternel de cette femme ce n'est qu'un virgule."

I then enquired after my friends Dubois and Fanchon.—He told me, that his mother had settled them at her house in the country, where she herself chose, of late, to pass at least one half of the year; that Dubois was of great service to her, in the quality of steward, and she had taken a strong affection for Fanchon, and that both husband and wife were loved and esteemed by the whole neighbourhood. "I once," continued the Marquis, "proposed to Fanchon, en badinant, to make a trip to Paris, for she must be tired of so much solitude." "Have I not my husband?" said she, "Your husband is not company," rejoined I, "your husband, you know, is yourself. What do you think was her answer?" "Elle m'a répondu," continued the Marquis, "Ah, Monsieur le Marquis, plus on sé loigne de soi-même, plus on s'écarte du bonheur."

In the progress of our conversation, I enquired about the lady to whom he was to have been married, when the match was so abruptly broken off by her father. He told me, the old gentleman's behaviour was explained a short time after our departure from Paris, by his daughter's marriage to a man of great fortune; but whose taste, character, and turn of mind were essentially different from those of the young lady. "I suppose then," said I, "she appeared indifferent about him from the beginning." "Pardonnez moi," replied the Marquis, "au commencement elle joua la belle passion pour son mari, jusqu'à scandaliser le monde, peu à peu elle devint plus raisonable, et sur cet article les deux epoux jouèrent bientôt à fortune égale, à présent ils s'amusent à se chicaner de petites contradictions qui jettent plus d'amertume dans le commerce que de torts décidés."

"Did you ever renew your acquaintance?"

"Je ne pouvois faire autrement, elle a marqué quelques petits regrets de m'avoir traité si cruellement."

"And how did you like her," said I, "on farther acquaintance?"

"Je lui ai trouvé," answered he, "tout ce qu'on pent souhaiter dans *la femme d'un autre*."

The Marquis, feeling himself a little cold, and rising from the sopha to ring for some wood, had a view of the street. "O ho," cried he, looking earnestly through the window, "regardez, regardez cet homme"—"Quel homme?" said I. "Cet homme à gros ventre," said he; and while he spoke, his teeth began to chatter. "Ah, Diable, voilà mon chien d'accés—cet homme qui marche comme un Di—Di—Dindon, c'est l'aumonier du regiment." I begged he would allow himself to be put to bed, for by this time he was all over shivering with the violence of the ague.

"Non, non, ce n'est rien," said he, "il faut absolument que je vous conte cette histoire. Cet homme qui s'engraisse en nettoy—nett—et—et—en nettoyant l'ame de mes soldats, faisoit les yeux doux à la femme d'un Ca—Ca—Caporal—Diantre je n'en peux plus. Adieu, mon ami, c'est la plus plaisante hist—sis—peste! demandez mes gens."

He was put to bed directly. I found the court below full of soldiers, who had come to enquire after their Colonel. Before I had reached the street, the Marquis's Valet-de-Chambre overtook me, le ris sur la bouche, et les larmes aux yeux, with a message from his master.

The soldiers crowded about us, with anxiety on all their countenances. I assured them, there was no danger; that their Colonel would be well within a very few days. This was heard with every mark of joy, and they dispersed, to communicate the good news to their comrades.

"Ah, Monsieur," said the Valet, addressing himself to me, "il est tant aimé de ces braves Garçons! et il merite si bien de l'être!"

Next day he looked better, and was in his usual spirits; the day following, he was still better; and having taken a proper quantity of the bark during the interval, he had no return of the fever. As he has promised to continue the use of the bark, in sufficient doses, for some time, and as relapses are not frequent at this season of the year, I am persuaded the affair is over, and that he will gradually gain strength till he is perfectly recovered.

He received me with less gaiety than usual, the day on which I took my leave, and used many obliging expressions, which, however you may smile, I am entirely disposed to believe were sincere; for

Altho' the candy'd tongue lick absurd pomp,

And crook the pregnant hinges of the knee,

Where thrift may follow fawning:

——Why should the poor be flatter'd?

Just as I was returning, we heard the music of the troops marching off the parade.——"Apropos," cried he, "How do your affairs go on with your Colonies?" I said, I hoped every thing would be arranged and settled very soon.

"Ne croyez vous pas," said he, "que ces Messieurs," pointing to the troops which then passed below the window, "pourroient entrer pour quelque chose dans l'arrangement?"

I said, I did not imagine the Americans were such fools as to break all connection with their friends, and then risk falling into the power of their enemies.

"Il me semble," answered he, "que ces Messieurs font assez peu de cas de votre amitié, et aussi, quand vous aurez prouvé qu'ils ont tort, il ne s'en suivra pas que vous ayiez toujours eu raison." "Allons," continued he, seeing that I looked a little grave, "point d'humeur;" then seizing my hand, "permettez moi, je vous prie, d'aimer les Anglois sans haïr les Américains."

I soon after parted with this amiable Frenchman, whose gaiety, wit, and agreeable manners, if I may judge from my own experience, represent the character and disposition of great numbers of his countrymen.

After a very agreeable journey by Gray, Langres, and Troyes, we arrived at this capital a few days ago.

LETTER LXXXII.

Paris.

Although it is a considerable time since my arrival, yet, as you made so long a stay at Paris while we were in Germany, I could not think of resuming my observations on the manners of this gay metropolis. It has been said, that those times are the most interesting to read of, which were the most disagreeable to live in. So I find the places in which it is most agreeable to reside, are precisely those from which we have the least inclination to write. There are so many resources at Paris, that it always requires a great effort to write letters, of any considerable length, from such a place. This is peculiarly my case at present, as I have the happiness of passing great part of my time with Mr. A—— S——t, whom I found at this hotel on my arrival. The integrity, candour, and ability, of that gentleman's conduct, during a long residence, have procured him a great number of friends in this capital, and have established a character which calumny attempted in vain to overthrow. Now that I have resolution to take up my pen, I shall endeavour to clear the debt for which you dun me so unmercifully. I own, I am surprised, that you should require my opinion on the uses of foreign travel, after perusing, as you must have done, the Dialogues, lately published by an eminent divine, equally distinguished for his learning and taste. But as I know what makes you peculiarly solicitous on that subject at present, I shall give you my sentiments, such as they are, without farther hesitation.

I cannot help thinking, that a young man of fortune may spend a few years to advantage, in travelling through some of the principal countries of Europe, provided the tour be well-timed, and well-conducted; and, without these, what part of education can be of use?

In a former letter, I gave my reasons for preferring the plan of education at the public schools of England, to any other now in use at home or abroad. After the young person has acquired the fundamental parts of learning, which are taught at schools, he will naturally be removed to some university. One of the most elegant and most ingenious writers of the present age has, in his Inquiry into the Causes of the Wealth of Nations, pointed out many deficiencies in those seminaries. What that gentleman has said on this subject, may possibly have some effect in bringing about an improvement. But, with all their deficiencies, it must be acknowledged, that no universities have produced a greater number of men distinguished for polite literature, and eminent for science, than those of England. If a young man has, previously, acquired the habit of application, and a taste for learning, he will certainly find the means of improvement there; and, without these, I know not where he will make any progress in literature. But whatever plan is adopted, whether the young man studies at the university, or at home with private teachers, while he is studying with diligence and alacrity, it would be doing him a most essential injury, to interrupt him by a premature expedition to the Continent, from an idea of his acquiring the graces, elegance of manner, or any of the accomplishments which travelling is supposed to give. Literature is preferable to all other accomplishments, and the men of rank who possess it, have a superiority over those who do not, let their graces be what they may, which the latter feel and envy, while they affect to despise.

According to this plan, a youth, properly educated, will seldom begin his foreign tour before the age of twenty; if it is a year or two later, there will be no harm.

This is the age, it may be said, when young men of fortune endeavour to get into Parliament: it is so; but if they should remain out of Parliament till they are a few years older, the affairs of the nation might possibly go on as well.

It may also be said, if the tour is deferred till the age of twenty, the youth will not, after that period of life, attain the modern languages in perfection. Nor will he acquire that easy manner, and fine address, which are only caught by an early acquaintance with courts, and the assemblies of the gay and elegant. This is true to a certain degree; but the answer is, that by remaining at home, and applying to the pursuits of literature, he will make more valuable attainments.

I am at a loss what to say about those same graces; it is certainly desirable to possess them, but they must come, as it were, spontaneously, or they will not come at all. They sometimes appear as volunteers, but cannot be pressed into any service; and those who shew the greatest anxiety about them, are the least likely to attain them. I should be cautious, therefore, of advising a young man to study them either at home or abroad with much solicitude. Students of the graces are, generally, the most abominably affected fellows in the world. I have seen *one* of them make a whole company squeamish.

Though the pert familiarity of French children would not become an English boy, yet it merits the earliest and the utmost attention to prevent or conquer that aukward timidity which so often oppresses the latter when he comes into company. The timidity I speak of, is entirely different from modesty. I have seen the most impudent boys I ever knew, almost convulsed with constraint in the presence of strangers, or when they were required to pronounce a single sentence of civility. But it was only on such occasions they were bashful. Among their companions or inferiors, they were saucy, rude, and boisterous.

If boys of this description *only* were liable to bashfulness, it would be a pity to remove it. But although this quality is distinct from modesty, it is not

npatible with it. Boys of the most modest and most amiable disposition
ften overwhelmed with it; from them it ought to be removed, if it can
one, without endangering that modesty which is so great an ornament to
th, and indeed to every period of life. This, surely, may be done in
gland, as well as in any other country; but it is too much neglected: many
nsider it as a matter of no importance, or that it will wear off by time. We
e it, however, often annihilate, and always impair the effect of the greatest
id most useful talents. After the care of forming the heart by the principles
f benevolence and integrity, perhaps one of the most important parts of
ducation is, to habituate a boy to behave with modesty, but without
restraint, and to retain the full possession of all his faculties in any company.

To attain, betimes, that ease and elegance of manner, which travelling is
supposed to bestow, and that the young gentleman may become perfectly
master of the modern languages, some have thought of mixing the two plans;
and, instead of allowing him to prosecute his studies at home, sending him
abroad, immediately on his coming from school, on the supposition that,
with the assistance of a tutor and foreign professors, he will proceed in the
study of philosophy, and other branches of literature, during the three or
four years which are employed in the usual tour. It will not be denied, that a
young man who has made good use of his time at school and at the university,
who has acquired such a taste for science as to consider its pursuits as a
pleasure, and not a task, may, even during his travels, mix the study of men
with that of books, and continue to make progress in the latter, when the
greater part of his time is dedicated to the former. But that such a taste will,
for *the first time*, spring up in the breast of a boy of sixteen or seventeen, amidst
the dissipation of theatres, reviews, processions, balls, and assemblies, is of
all things the least probable.

Others, who think lightly of the importance of what is usually called science
to a young man of rank and fortune, still contend, that a knowledge of
history, which they admit may be of some use *even to men of fortune*, can
certainly be acquired during the years of travelling. But what sort of a
knowledge will it be which a boy, in such a situation, will acquire? Not that
which Lord Bolingbroke calls philosophy, teaching by examples, a proper
conduct in the various situations of public and private life, but merely a
succession of reigns, of battles, and sieges, stored up in the memory without
reflection or application. I remember a young gentleman, whom a strong and
retentive memory of such events often set a prating very mal-à-propos; one
of his companions expressed much surprise at his knowledge, and wondered
how he had laid up such a store. "Why, truly," replied he, with frankness, "it
is all owing to my bungling blockhead of a valet, who takes up such an
unconscionable time in dressing my hair, that I am glad to read to keep me

from fretting; and as there are no newspapers, or magazines, to be had in this country, I have been driven to history, which answers nearly as well."

But it sometimes happens, that young men who are far behind their contemporaries in every kind of literature, are wonderfully advanced in the knowledge of the town, so as to vie with the oldest professors in London, and endanger their own health by the ardour of their application. The sooner such premature youths are separated from the connections they have formed in the metropolis, the better; and as it will not be easy to persuade them to live in any other part of Great Britain, it will be necessary to send them abroad. But, instead of being carried to courts and capitals, the best plan for them will be, to fix them in some provincial town of France or Switzerland, where they may have a chance of improving, not so much by new attainments, as by unlearning or forgetting what they have already acquired.

After a young man has employed his time to advantage at a public school, and has continued his application to various branches of science till the age of twenty, you ask, what are the advantages he is likely to reap from a tour abroad?

He will see mankind more at large, and in numberless situations and points of view, in which they cannot appear in Great Britain, or any one country. By comparing the various customs and usages, and hearing the received opinions of different countries, his mind will be enlarged. He will be enabled to correct the theoretical notions he may have formed of human nature, by the practical knowledge of men. By contemplating their various religions, laws, and government, *in action*, as it were, and observing the effects they produce on the minds and characters of the people, he will be able to form a juster estimate of their value than otherwise he could have done. He will see the natives of other countries, not as he sees them in England, mere idle spectators, but busily employed in their various characters, as actors on their own proper stage. He will gradually improve in the knowledge of *character*, not of Englishmen only, but of men in general; he will cease to be deceived either by the varnish with which men are apt to heighten their own actions, or the dark colours in which they, too often, paint those of others. He will learn to distinguish the real from the ostensible motive of men's words and behaviour. Finally, by being received with hospitality, conversing familiarly, and living in the reciprocal exchange of good offices with those whom he considered as enemies, or in some unfavourable point of view, the sphere of his benevolence and good-will to his brethren of mankind will gradually enlarge. His friendships extending beyond the limits, of his own country, will embrace characters congenial with his own in other nations. Seas, mountains, rivers, are *geographical* boundaries, but never limited the good-will or esteem of one liberal mind. As for his manner, though it will probably not be so janty as if he had been bred in France from his earliest youth, yet that also will in some degree be improved.

However persuaded he may be of the advantages enjoyed by the people of England, he will see the harshness and impropriety of insulting the natives of other countries with an ostentatious enumeration of those advantages; he will perceive how odious those travellers make themselves, who laugh at the religion, ridicule the customs, and insult the police of the countries through which they pass, and who never fail to insinuate to the inhabitants that they are all slaves and bigots. Such bold Britons we have sometimes met with, *fighting* their way through Europe, who, by their continual broils and disputes, would lead one to imagine that the angel of the Lord had pronounced on each of them the same denunciation which he did on Ishmael the son of Abraham, by his handmaid Hagar. "And he will be a wild man, and his hand will be against every man, and every man's hand against him[12]." If the same unsocial disposition should creep into our politics, it might arm all the powers in Europe against Great Britain, before she gets clear of her unhappy contest with America. A young man, whose mind has been formed as it ought, before he goes abroad, when he sees many individuals preserve personal dignity in spite of arbitrary government, an independent mind amidst poverty, liberal and philosophic sentiments amidst bigotry and superstition; must naturally have the highest esteem for such characters, and allow them more merit than those even of his own country, who think and act in the same manner in less unfavourable circumstances.

Besides these advantages, a young man of fortune, by spending a few years abroad, will gratify a natural and laudable curiosity, and pass a certain portion of his life in an agreeable manner. He will form an acquaintance with that boasted nation, whose superior taste and politeness are universally acknowledged; whose fashions and language are adopted by all Europe; and who, in science, power, and commerce, are the rivals of Great Britain. He will have opportunities of observing the political constitution of the German empire; that complex body, formed by a confederacy of princes, ecclesiastics, and free cities, comprehending countries of vast extent, inhabited by a hardy race of men, distinguished for solid sense and integrity, who, without having equalled their sprightlier neighbours in works of taste or imagination, have shewn what prodigious efforts of application the human mind is capable of in the severest and least amusing studies, and whose armies exhibit at present the most perfect models of military discipline. In contemplating these, he will naturally consider, whether those armies tend most to the aggrandizement of the Monarch, or to defend or preserve any thing to the people who maintain them, and the soldiers who compose them, equivalent to the vast expence of money, and the still greater quantity of misery which they occasion.

Viewing the remains of Roman taste and magnificence, he will feel a thousand emotions of the most interesting nature, while those whose minds are not, like his, stored with classical knowledge, gaze with tasteless wonder, or phlegmatic indifference; and, exclusive of those monuments of antiquity, he will naturally desire to be acquainted with the present inhabitants of a country, which at different periods has produced men who, by one means or another, have distinguished themselves so eminently from their contemporaries of other nations. At one period, having subdued the world by the wisdom and firmness of their councils, and the disciplined vigour of their armies, Rome became at once the seat of empire, learning, and the arts.

After the Northern barbarians had destroyed the overgrown fabric of Roman power, a new empire, of a more singular nature, gradually arose from its ruins, artfully extending its influence over the minds of men, till the Princes of Europe were at length as much controlled by the bulls of the Vatican, as their ancestors had been by the decrees of the Senate.

Commerce also, which rapine and slaughter had frightened from Europe, returned, and joined with Superstition in drawing the riches of all the neighbouring nations to Italy. And, at a subsequent period, Learning, bursting through the clouds of ignorance which overshadowed mankind, again shone forth in the same country, bringing in her train, Poetry, Painting, Sculpture, and Music, all of which have been cultivated with the greatest success; and the three last brought, by the inhabitants of this country, to a degree of excellence unequalled by the natives of any other country of the world. When to these considerations we add, that there is reason to believe that this country had arrived at a great degree of perfection in the arts before the beginning of the Roman republic, we are almost tempted to believe, that local and physical causes have a considerable influence in rendering the mind more acute in this country of Italy, than any where else; and that if the infinite political disadvantages under which it labours were removed, and the whole of this peninsula united in one State, it would again resume its superiority over other nations.

Lastly, by visiting other countries, a subject of Great Britain will acquire a greater esteem than ever for the constitution of his own. Freed from vulgar prejudices, he will perceive, that the blessings and advantages which his countrymen enjoy, do not flow from their superiority in wisdom, courage, or virtue, over the other nations of the world, but, in some degree, from the peculiarity of their situation in an island; and, above all, from those just and equitable laws which secure property, that mild free government which abhors tyranny, protects the meanest subject, and leaves the mind of man to its own exertions, unrestrained by those arbitrary, capricious, and impolitic shackles, which confine and weaken its noblest endeavours in almost every other country of the world. This animates industry, creates fertility, and scatters plenty over the boisterous island of Great Britain, with a profusion unknown in the neighbouring nations, who behold with astonishment such numbers of British subjects, of both sexes, and of all ages, roaming discontented through the lands of despotism, in search of that happiness, which, if satiety and the wanton restlessness of wealth would permit, they have a much better prospect of enjoying in their own country.

Cœlum non animum mutant qui trans mare currunt.

Strenua nos exercet inertia, navibus atque

Quadrigis petimus bene vivere. Quod petis, hic est.

[12] Vide Genesis, chap. xvi. verse 12.

THE END.

Milton Keynes UK
Ingram Content Group UK Ltd.
UKHW030852011224
451361UK00001B/62

9 789362 921871